CAKE
DECORATING
BOOK

Cover Photo: Cornucopia Cake 50

CAKE DECORATING

CAKE DECORATING BOOK

Phyllis Magida
Book designed by Margot L. Wolf
Illustrations by William H. Jones
Photography: Zdenek Piveka

BOOK

Culinary Arts Institute.

A DIVISION OF • DELAIR PUBLISHING COMPANY INC.

ISBN: 0-8326-0603-0

Contents

What is Cake Decorating?

There are many excellent cake-decorating books on the market, each showing the wonderful things you can do with a pastry tube once the technique is mastered. Cake decorating, though, should include more than just ways to use the pastry tube. To us, decoration means what it means in the dictionary: "To adorn with something ornamental." Every time you put something on a cake, or bake something into a cake, you are adorning (decorating) it.

Decorations, then, can range from the merest sprinkling of confectioners' sugar on an unfrosted cake to the elaborate mass of marzipan fruits spilling out of the cornucopia shown on the cover. Each has its place, and each is effective under the right circumstances.

This book has been written to cover those many occasions when decorated cakes would be more effective than plain ones. These range from picnics, where cakes may be festive but must be easy to wrap and transport, to children's parties, where cakes should be both fanciful yet simple enough for a child to assist in the decorating.

The decorations described have been worked out to cover a multitude of tastes, too. There are decorations for the manually untalented (Porcupine Cake, page 30, for the hurried (Lamb Cake, page 35, made from a mix), for the gourmet (Molded Chocolate Cake, page 44), and for the person who enjoys whole afternoons spent at the kitchen table modeling marzipan fruits and vegetables for future use (page 52).

But along with decorations, we have also concentrated on taste. So many cakes look wonderful and delicious—setting up all kinds of expectations which aren't satisfied when the cake is eaten. Cakes, we think, must taste as good as they look; otherwise the diners feel cheated. All of the cakes in this book, then, were chosen initially for their basic good taste; then we added icings that would both enhance the taste of the individual cakes, and at the same time, perform well as a medium for decoration.

One thing we're proud of is our economy. We didn't stint on ingredients, but we were terribly economical when it came to cake pans. We use only one special mold (Lamb Cake, page 30); the rest are standard sizes. We're especially proud too, of our heart, shamrock, and doll cakes, all made from sheet cakes with parts and layers cut out of them (see Patterns, pages 65-67). Most of the ingredients used in this book can be found easily at the supermarket.

Techniques that require a special description or "lesson" have been noted in the chapter introductions. Suggestions for baking well-formed decorative layers are found in Chapter 1. Chapter 2 explains frosting the cake. Chapter 3 explains techniques for using food coloring. Simple techniques for using the pastry tube and making your own parchment bag are in Chapter 4. Chapter 5 describes making full-blown icing roses, using the flower nail.

We have tried to make these "lessons" very clear and readable. And we hope that the illustrations, together with the written descriptions, make each technique easy to follow and understand.

Most important, we hope this book will add to your store of decorating ideas. The majority of decorating books ask you to read and then to work from them directly. But none so far have asked you, as we are doing, to create ideas of your own, by using our cakes and decorations as a guide. Tailor your cake and its decorations to your family, your guests, the occasion, and to your own taste.

Inside Decorated Cakes

The appearance of a cake, inside and out, contributes to the final effect. In this chapter, the decorating emphasis is on the inside of the cake. The outside is sometimes frosted as well, but this is partly to hide the surprise interior as well as to enhance the taste. I remember the tiny shock of pleasure I felt once, upon seeing what looked on the outside like a plain, frosted chocolate cake, turn out to have a checkerboard interior.

Several different interior patterns are included in this chapter. Sometimes the top section of a cake is sliced off and the inside hollowed out and stuffed with a rich filling before the top is replaced. Other cake interiors may be checkered or layered for a striped effect. One cake has a pinwheel for a middle layer; another is marbled and then topped with a hidden layer of melted marshmallows between the cake top and the chocolate icing.

Achieving good *interior* decorating is tied up, obviously, with good baking techniques. Besides the basic rules of baking, such as having all ingredients at room temperature, measuring exactly, using a preheated oven, we're including a few additional suggestions which might be helpful in achieving the desired results.

The one baking technique which gives even the experienced cook trouble is the folding process. In this, egg whites are beaten stiffly so that they're full of air; then these are introduced into the batter so as to aerate it. This results in a lightened and leavened cake, since heat causes the whites to expand and the cake rises proportionately.

Beaten egg whites are fragile, however; they lose air easily, especially when a heavy hand is used in folding. I use a tool called an egg whip (see illustration); it seems almost to incorporate the egg whites for you.

To fold, spoon the batter over the beaten whites (instead of vice versa) in order to handle the whites as little as possible. Fold by moving the egg whip or a rubber spatula down in the center of bowl to the bottom; then moving it toward you along the bottom of bowl, then up the side in front of you. Repeat, after giving the bowl a small turn to the left (see illustration). Continue making similar strokes, and turning the bowl a few degrees after each stroke, until only a few unmixed patches remain. Use as few strokes as possible. Then immediately spoon the batter into prepared pans and put in the oven at once.

Cake pans should be well greased and lined on the bottom with greased parchment paper. This will allow the cake to come out of the pan intact, with none clinging to the pan bottom. This step is doubly important since it's the underside of the cake, the part that touches the pan bottom while baking, that gets the frosting.

Parchment paper circles (but not squares or rectangles) are available in a number of sizes, or you can buy a roll of parchment paper and cut shapes to fit your pan bottoms.

Another suggestion for achieving attractive cakes is to remember to fill the baking pans not more than two thirds full of batter, or you take the chance of the batter spilling over the top and falling to the oven floor. If you want a higher cake than your pan sides allow, fold a length of aluminum foil in half lengthwise and press it around the sides of pan so it extends upward past the top, like a paper collar tied around a souffle dish. Tie a piece of string tightly around the foil to secure. This collar also helps the layers to bake more evenly.

Another way to do this is to use a rubber spatula to level the batter. In round pans, the layers often bake with high centers, so push the batter toward the sides. In square pans, the layers often bake with concave centers, so push the batter away from sides and into the center.

Cakes that bake unevenly can be leveled when chilled (or frozen) by sawing off the uneven part, a little at a time, with a long-bladed, serrated knife. If the right side of the cake is too high, for example, saw it off in thin layers; don't try to cut it off all at once. If you wish, commercial cake levelers are also available.

Cakes should be baked and cooled completely before frosting is added. Although most cakes taste best on the day they're made, frosting will go on more easily if the cake is not absolutely fresh.

To freeze: Multilayered cakes should be filled and frozen, but most people are happier with layers that are frozen without frosting. On serving day, they can easily be filled and frosted.

Remember to wrap and seal cakes very carefully before putting them in the freezer. Wrap cakes securely in waxed paper, freezer paper, or aluminum foil. Then put them in a plastic bag with a twister seal. To prevent freezer taste, don't freeze longer than two months.

•

The cake for the center layer of this three-layer cake is baked in a jelly-roll pan, then is frosted and cut into strips that are rolled around each other to form a large pinwheel. The pinwheel effect shows up when the cake is cut into pieces. ►

Pinwheel Sponge Cake

  6 **egg yolks**
  ³/₄ **cup sugar**
  6 **tablespoons water**
  2¹/₄ **teaspoons vanilla extract**
  1¹/₂ **cups sifted cake flour**
  6 **egg whites**
  ³/₄ **teaspoon cream of tartar**
  ¹/₄ **teaspoon salt**
  ³/₄ **cup sugar**
    Confectioners' sugar
    Mocha-Chocolate Buttercream
  1 **cup chopped pecans**

1. Grease bottom of a 15x10x1-inch jelly-roll pan and two 8-inch round layer cake pans; line them with waxed paper cut to fit bottom of pans; grease paper. Set aside.

2. Beat egg yolks, ³/₄ cup sugar, water, and vanilla extract together in a small bowl until very thick. Fold in flour until just blended.

3. Beat egg whites with cream of tartar and salt in a large bowl until frothy. Add ³/₄ cup sugar gradually, continuing to beat until stiff peaks are formed.

4. Fold egg yolk mixture into meringue until blended. Turn batter into the prepared pans (4 cups of batter for jelly-roll pan and 2 cups each for round layer cake pans); spread evenly.

5. Bake at 325°F 20 to 25 minutes, or until cake tests done.

6. Loosen cake from pans. Immediately turn sheet cake onto a towel with confectioners' sugar sifted over it. Peel off the paper and trim any crisp edges of cake. Turn layers onto wire racks and peel off paper.

7. Roll up sheet cake, beginning at one end of

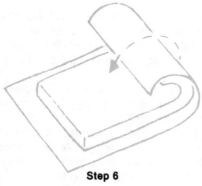

Step 6

Step 7

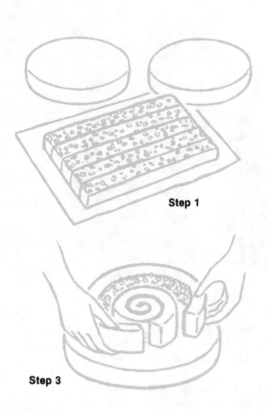

Step 1

Step 3

cake. Using the towel as a guide, tightly grasp nearest edge of towel and quickly pull it over beyond opposite edge. Cake will roll itself as you pull. Wrap roll in towel and set on wire rack to cool about 30 minutes.

8. When ready to frost and fill, carefully unroll cooled cake and spread thickly with Mocha-Chocolate Buttercream. Sprinkle with ⅓ cup chopped pecans. Assemble as directed below, using frosting and remaining chopped pecans. Cover top and sides of cake with remaining frosting and decorate, if desired, with additional chopped pecans.

One 3-layer 8-inch cake

TO ASSEMBLE PINWHEEL CAKE

1. Cut frosted cake into 6 lengthwise strips, about 1½ inches wide (see illustration).
2. Place one 8-inch round cake layer on a cake plate; spread with buttercream and sprinkle with ⅓ cup chopped pecans.
3. Roll up one jelly-roll strip into a pinwheel and place in center of frosted layer (see illustration).
4. Roll all remaining strips loosely around center pinwheel until pinwheel covers whole bottom layer.
5. Spread remaining 8-inch layer with frosting and sprinkle with remaining ⅓ cup chopped pecans. Place layer on top of pinwheel, frosted side down.

Mocha-Chocolate Buttercream

12 ounces semisweet chocolate
½ cup strong coffee
3 cups firm unsalted butter
2 tablespoons liqueur such as kirsch, curacao, or Cointreau
1½ cups light corn syrup
8 egg yolks

1. Put chocolate and coffee into the top of a double boiler. Set over hot (not simmering) water until chocolate is melted; blend well. Set aside to cool.
2. Cream butter and liqueur until light and fluffy; set aside.
3. Pour corn syrup into a saucepan. Set candy thermometer in place. Boil corn syrup gently to 230° to 234°F (thread stage).
4. Meanwhile, beat the egg yolks until very thick. Continue beating constantly while pouring syrup very slowly into egg yolks. Beat until mixture is very thick and of same consistency as the whipped butter. Cool completely.
5. Beat egg yolk mixture, about 2 tablespoons at a time, into butter until just blended. Gradually blend in the chocolate. (If tightly covered, this frosting may be stored for several days in refrigerator.)

About 6 cups frosting

The folowing cake, invented by the Dutch in Indonesia, combines Dutch flour and dairy products with Indonesian spices. The alternating dark and light layers are added and baked one by one. As the layers bake they adhere to each other, giving the cake a striped effect when it is cut into pieces.

This dessert, always a conversation piece, will become a favorite as soon as you get used to its odd but very interesting spongy texture. Traditional Indonesian cake has 18 thin/thin layers. We have baked ours in six thicker layers.

Indonesian Striped Spice Cake (Spek Koek)

14	tablespoons butter
1½	cups sugar
8	egg yolks
1	teaspoon vanilla extract
1¼	cups all-purpose flour
½	teaspoon salt
2½	teaspoons cinnamon
1¼	teaspoons nutmeg
1	teaspoon ginger
½	teaspoon cardamom
¼	teaspoon allspice
¼	teaspoon cloves
⅛	teaspoon mace
8	egg whites
	Melted butter (about ¾ cup)
	Confectioners' sugar for sprinkling

1. Grease bottom of a 9-inch springform pan and line the bottom with a circle of waxed or parchment paper cut to fit; grease paper.

2. Cream butter with sugar until well blended; add yolks and vanilla extract and beat well. Then add flour and salt and beat until well mixed.

3. Spoon half of batter into a separate bowl and add a blend of the spices; mix well.

4. Beat egg whites until peaks are stiff, but not dry. Divide in half and fold half into each portion of batter.

5. Spoon 1 cup of dark batter onto bottom of prepared pan to form a thin layer.

6. Set pan on lowest rack of oven.

7. Bake at 325°F about 20 minutes, or until layer tests done.

8. Remove pan from oven and use a pastry brush to spread a very thin layer of melted butter over top of baked layer. Then spoon 1 cup light batter over top of baked layer and return to oven until layer tests done (about 20 minutes). Brush top with melted butter as before.

9. Continue to alternate light and dark layers, brushing each baked layer with melted butter, until all batter is used and cake is 6 layers thick. When last layer is added, return cake to oven and bake until center tests done and cake top is nicely browned (25 to 30 minutes).

10. Remove side of springform and set cake on wire rack to cool. When cool, remove springform bottom and wrap cake in foil, securing tightly. Store wrapped cake in a container with a tight-fitting lid and allow it to ripen for 2 days before serving.

11. At serving time, place cake on a serving plate and dust top with confectioners' sugar, if desired. Serve, cut in small pieces. Cake will keep up to 2 weeks if stored as directed.

One 9-inch cake

●

The following cake is made in what the Viennese call Indian style—a tall, single-layer cake is baked; then a thin layer is sliced off horizontally, about ½ inch from the top. The center is hollowed out and filled with some kind of mousse or Chantilly cream in a contrasting color.

Some versions of this cake are baked in a tube pan, which gives an interesting tunnel effect; in others the top is covered with a rich frosting, or the filled cake is served with a thick, sweet dessert sauce on the side. But our version, baked in a springform pan, is so good by itself that we think any extra sauce or icing would be gilding the chocolate lily.

●

Chocolate Indianer

4½ ounces (4½ squares) unsweetened chocolate
1 cup butter
2¼ cups sugar
4 eggs
1 teaspoon vanilla extract
1¼ cups buttermilk
1 cup milk
3⅓ cups sifted cake flour
1 tablespoon baking powder
1 teaspoon baking soda
¼ teaspoon salt
2 tablespoons rum
Indianer Filling
Confectioners' sugar for sprinkling on top of cake

1. Butter the bottom and sides of a 10-inch springform pan.
2. Melt chocolate in the top of a double boiler. Set aside to cool.
3. In large bowl of electric mixer, beat butter until softened, then add sugar, creaming well. Add eggs, one at a time, beating well after each addition. Beat melted chocolate into mixture along with vanilla extract.
4. Mix buttermilk with milk. Sift flour with baking powder, baking soda, and salt. Add buttermilk mixture to batter alternately with dry ingredients, beating well after each addition. Turn batter into prepared springform pan and spread evenly.
5. Bake at 350°F 1 hour and 40 minutes, or until cake tests done. Remove cake from oven and set aside 10 minutes, then release side of springform. Set cake, still on springform bottom, on wire rack and allow to cool.
6. With a long-bladed, serrated knife, slice off top of cake horizontally, just under the rim. Set top aside. Using a small, sharp knife, cut out center of cake, leaving a ¹/₂-inch rim. Hollow out cake about 1¹/₄ inches deep and sprinkle inside with rum. (Use extra cake as desired.)
7. Shortly before serving time, make filling, then spoon filling into hollow of cake, packing it tightly and smoothly; replace top of cake. Use a sugar shaker to sprinkle top evenly with confectioners' sugar. Or rub some confectioners' sugar through a sieve onto top of cake if no shaker is available. Serve immediately, or store in refrigerator until serving time.

One 10-inch filled cake

Indianer Filling

2 **cups whipping cream**
1/2 **cup confectioners' sugar**
2 **cups chopped walnuts**
1/4 **cup rum**

Whip cream until it begins to stiffen. With beaters still running, add confectioners' sugar, 1 tablespoon at a time. Then turn off beaters and stir in walnuts and rum. Use immediately to fill Chocolate Indianer.

The Punch Cake, a famous Viennese dessert, is similar to Chocolate Indianer. One cake layer is sliced in half for the top and bottom layers of the cake. The center of the other cake layer is hollowed out, then the cake taken from the center is soaked in a sweet, fruity syrup and packed into the hollow. The top is set in place and the cake is weighted down. Finally, the cake is covered with a pink icing.

Punch Cake

Sponge Cake
3 **tablespoons sieved apricot jam**
1 **tablespoon dark rum**
Punch Syrup
Punch Icing

1. With a long-bladed, serrated knife, slice 1 cooled sponge cake layer horizontally in half. Set the bottom slice on bottom of an 8-inch springform pan; set top slice aside.
2. Mix apricot jam and rum; spread lightly over cake slice on pan bottom. Reserve remaining jam.
3. With a small, sharp knife, cut out center of remaining cake layer, leaving about a 1-inch border. Set cake ring on jam-spread cake; spread remaining jam on ring. Cut cake removed from center into 1/2-inch cubes and put into a bowl. Pour Punch Syrup over cake cubes and toss lightly to combine until cake has absorbed all liquid.
4. Fill cake hollow with saturated cake, packing it in so that all is used; top with reserved cake slice and

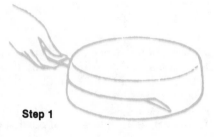

Step 1

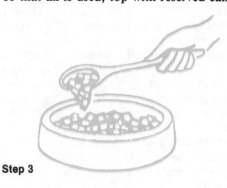

Step 3

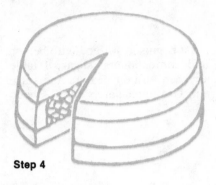

Step 4

put side on springform pan. Set a flat round layer cake pan, the same size as the cake, on top of the cake and place a brick or heavy object in the pan to weight the cake down. Do not remove weight for 4 hours.

5. After removing weight, place cake on a serving plate and pour Punch Icing over top, allowing it to run down sides. Spread icing to cover sides, then refrigerate cake until serving time.

One 8-inch cake

Sponge Cake

    7 egg yolks
    1 cup sugar
    7 tablespoons water
2½ teaspoons vanilla extract
1¾ cups sifted cake flour
    7 egg whites
  ¾ teaspoon cream of tartar
  ¼ teaspoon salt
  ¾ cup sugar

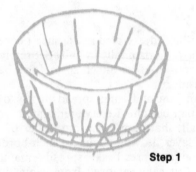

Step 1

1. Grease bottoms and sides of two 8-inch round layer cake pans; line bottoms with parchment paper and grease paper. Tear off a 3-foot length of aluminum foil, cut in half lengthwise, fold each piece in half lengthwise, and grease the foil. Press foil around rim to secure, then tie it around the pans, greased side in, in a manner similar to a paper collar tied around a souffle dish.

2. Beat egg yolks, sugar, water, and vanilla extract together until very thick. Fold in flour until just blended. Beat egg whites with cream of tartar and salt until frothy. Add ¾ cup sugar gradually, continuing to beat until stiff peaks are formed.

3. Fold egg yolk mixture into meringue until blended. Turn batter into prepared pans and spread evenly.

4. Bake at 350°F 45 minutes, or until cake tests done. Carefully remove foil collars; loosen cake from pans and turn cakes upside down onto wire racks. Remove parchment paper and cool layers right side up on racks.

2 high 8-inch round cake layers

Punch Syrup

  ½ cup sugar
  ½ cup water
1½ teaspoons freshly grated orange
       peel
1½ teaspoons freshly grated lemon
       peel
    3 tablespoons strained fresh
         orange juice
    3 tablespoons strained fresh lemon
         juice
    6 tablespoons dark rum
    1 to 2 tablespoons coarsely
         chopped or grated semisweet
         chocolate
    2 drops red food coloring

1. Bring sugar, water, orange peel, and lemon peel to boiling in a saucepan and cook until candy thermometer registers 234° to 236°F, or until mixture forms a soft ball in cold water.

2. Add orange and lemon juices, return to boiling, and remove from heat. Pour into a small bowl and let cool.

3. When mixture has cooled, stir in rum, chocolate, and food coloring.

Punch Icing

1   egg white
1½ cups confectioners' sugar
1   tablespoon butter, melted
2   tablespoons sieved apricot jam
    Dark rum (about 2 tablespoons)
    Red food coloring (about 6 drops)

Beat egg white until frothy in small bowl of electric mixer. Beat in confectioners' sugar, butter, jam, and enough rum for good spreading consistency. Blend in enough food coloring to tint icing pink.

1 cup icing

•

The following five-layer cake is made of special meringue called *broyage* in which ground nuts and cornstarch replace some of the sugar; the nuts add flavor and the cornstarch adds body. *Broyage* is crisp immediately after baking, but if spread with filling and refrigerated for twenty-four hours before serving, the layers will soften to a delicious, chewy texture.

Some years ago, gourmet Michael Field discovered that a small amount of powder called calcium phosphate would stop meringues from seeping sugar, or "weeping," if it was added before baking. The proportion he used was ½ teaspoon calcium phosphate powder to 4 egg whites.

Since calcium phosphate powder is sold over drugstore counters as a calcium diet supplement, there's no reason why it shouldn't be included optionally in the following recipe. If purchased in pill form, the pills may be crushed to a powder; if bought in capsules, then simply open the capsules and shake the powder out into a small bowl and measure. Calcium phosphate powder can be used successfully in every kind of meringue, from pie topping to vacherin.

•

Broyage Cake

Meringue Layers
Coffee Buttercream (page 26)

1. One or two days before serving, assemble cake, using Meringue Layers and Coffee Buttercream. Place a meringue layer on a serving plate and spread amply with buttercream (about ½ cup). Top with second layer and repeat with same amount of frosting. Continue with layers and frosting until top layer is added, but do not frost.

2. Use about half of remaining frosting to frost sides of cake. Put remaining frosting in a pastry bag with a large star tube and pipe 2 rows of rosettes (instructions, page 58) around top of cake. Refrigerate for at least a day before serving. Store cake in refrigerator under foil tent, if possible.

1 layered 8-inch cake

Simple Outside Decorated Cake 28
Dobos Torte 22

Meringue Layers

6 egg whites
½ teaspoon cream of tartar
⅛ teaspoon salt
¾ teaspoon calcium phosphate
    powder (optional)
2 teaspoons vanilla extract
1⅓ cups sugar
½ cup ground almonds
½ cup cornstarch

1. In large bowl of electric mixer, beat egg whites until they hold soft peaks. Then add cream of tartar, salt, and calcium phosphate powder and beat for a few seconds. Add vanilla extract and beat again, then beat in 1 cup sugar, a tablespoon at a time, until mixture is very stiff. Turn mixer off.

2. Meanwhile, in a small bowl, combine remaining ⅓ cup sugar with ground nuts and cornstarch. Fold mixture into meringue until well combined. There will be about 6 cups batter.

3. Grease and flour large cookie sheets and trace five 8-inch circles in the pan coating. Fill each circle with a generous 1 cup meringue, then use a rubber spatula to ease meringue out to edges.

4. Bake at 200°F 1 hour. Turn off oven and let dry until meringue feels perfectly dry to the touch (at least 4 hours, or preferably overnight). Remove from oven and use a long, flat-bladed knife to loosen meringues from pans.

5. Use a small, sharp knife and scissors to trim any rough edges, if needed; work carefully as material is very brittle. Carefully wrap layers and store.

5 meringue layers

Checkerboard cakes are usually made in three layers, each using two different-colored and different-flavored batters in alternating rings or squares. The layers are then assembled and the cake frosted. When the cake is cut into, it gives a checkerboard effect.

A nice checkerboard cake is possible, however, without using special forms. Both the chocolate and spice cakes below are baked in four layers—two light and two dark—and the center and middle sections of each are lifted out and interchanged (see illustrations).

Chocolate Checkerboard Cake

2½ ounces (2½ squares)
    unsweetened chocolate
¾ cup butter
1 tablespoon vanilla extract
1½ cups sugar
3 cups sifted cake flour
1 tablespoon baking powder
¾ teaspoon salt
1 cup plus 2 tablespoons milk
3 tablespoons hot water
1½ tablespoons sugar
¾ teaspoon baking soda
4 egg whites

1. Melt chocolate in top of a double boiler.

2. Meanwhile, cream butter with vanilla extract and 1½ cups sugar in a bowl. Mix flour, baking powder, and salt; add alternately with milk to the creamed mixture, beating until blended. Spoon a little more than half of batter into a separate bowl. Set aside.

3. To batter in first bowl, add melted chocolate, hot water, remaining 1½ tablespoons sugar, and baking soda; mix well. (See Note.)

4. Beat egg whites until peaks are stiff, but not dry. Fold half into chocolate batter and half into white batter.

1 jar (16 ounces) apricot
    preserves, pureed in blender
    (or substitute raspberry jam,
    pressed through sieve to
    remove seeds)
Chocolate Fudge Frosting

Step 2

Step 3

Step 4

5. Divide chocolate batter evenly between 2 greased 8-inch round layer cake or square baking pans; then divide white batter between 2 greased 8-inch round layer cake or square baking pans.*

6. Bake at 350°F about 20 minutes, or until cake tests done. Cool 5 minutes in pans, then turn layers out on wire racks to cool. Assemble as directed below, putting sections and layers together with pureed jam. Refrigerate assembled cake until chilled, then frost with Chocolate Fudge Frosting.

One 4-layer 8-inch cake

Note: If you have only 2 pans of either shape or size, bake the dark layers first, then empty the pans and bake the white layers. Remember though, that beaten egg whites fall if left standing, so divide unbeaten whites in half. Beat first half, add to chocolate batter, and bake; when ready to bake white layers, beat second half of egg whites, fold into white batter, and bake as directed.

TO ASSEMBLE CHECKERBOARD CAKE

1. Depending on the size and shape of the cake baked, make squares or circles on tracing paper and cut out shapes; then use them to make cardboard patterns.

2. Lay the larger of the cardboard patterns (large square or circle) on each of the four layers (see illustration) and use a serrated knife to cut around it carefully. Remove these middle sections from each layer.

3. Lay the smaller of the cardboard patterns (small square or circle) on each middle section (the one just removed) and cut around it carefully; then remove all these center sections (see illustration).

4. There should be four outer borders, four middle pieces, and four center pieces. Set one dark border on a cake plate and spread cut surfaces with jam. Set light middle section in place and spread cut surfaces with jam. Then set dark center section in place. Paint top of layer with jam. (See illustration.)

5. Set one light border on top of assembled layer and paint cut surfaces with jam. Insert dark middle section, paint with jam as before, and set light center in place. Cover this layer with jam, also. Repeat with remaining layers, using dark border for third layer and light border for top. Coat top of cake with a layer of jam.

---

*Four thin 8-inch round layers bake in the same length of time as 4 slightly thinner square layers. Or, if desired, you might bake the cake in 6 round layers for an elaborate checkerboard effect. Square layers are too thin to bake in 6 layers unless batter is increased.

Chocolate Fudge Frosting

3 ounces (3 squares) unsweetened chocolate, cut in pieces
2 cups sugar
⅔ cup milk
⅓ cup butter or margarine
4 teaspoons light corn syrup
2 teaspoons vanilla extract

1. Combine all ingredients except vanilla extract in a heavy 3-quart saucepan. Heat slowly, stirring until sugar is dissolved. Bring rapidly to boiling.
2. Set candy thermometer in place and cook, stirring occasionally, to 234°F (soft-ball stage; remove from heat while testing). Using a pastry brush dipped in water, wash down the crystals from sides of saucepan from time to time during cooking.
3. Remove from heat and cool to 110°F without stirring or jarring. Then mix in vanilla extract. Beat until of spreading consistency.

About 2 cups frosting

Spice Checkerboard Cake

5 eggs, separated
3 egg whites
½ cup salad oil
¾ cup water
2¼ cups sifted cake flour
1 tablespoon baking powder
¾ teaspoon salt
1 cup lightly packed dark brown sugar
½ teaspoon cinnamon
¼ teaspoon allspice
¼ teaspoon cloves
¼ teaspoon nutmeg
Pinch ginger
¾ cup granulated sugar
1 teaspoon vanilla extract
½ teaspoon cream of tartar
1 jar (16 ounces) apricot preserves, pureed in blender
Brown Sugar Seven-Minute Frosting

1. Put egg yolks and 8 egg whites into separate bowls; set whites aside. Combine egg yolks, salad oil, and water. Mix flour, baking powder, and salt; add in 4 portions to egg yolk mixture, beating well after each addition. Spoon half of batter into a separate bowl.
2. To batter in first bowl, add brown sugar and spices; mix well. To batter in second bowl, add granulated sugar and vanilla extract; mix well. (See Note with Chocolate Checkerboard Cake, page 19).
3. Beat egg whites and cream of tartar until peaks are stiff, but not dry. Divide beaten whites between the 2 batters and fold until blended.
4. Divide spice batter between two well-greased and floured 9-inch round layer cake or square baking pans, then do the same with light batter.
5. Bake at 350°F 15 to 20 minutes, or until cake tests done.
6. Turn layers upside down on wire racks until cool.
7. If layers have not fallen out, use a knife to ease layers out of pans. When cool, cut and assemble layers as directed above, putting them together with pureed jam. Refrigerate assembled cake until chilled, then frost with Brown Sugar Seven-Minute Frosting.

One 4-layer 9-inch cake

Brown Sugar Seven-Minute Frosting

¾ **cup firmly packed dark brown sugar**
¾ **cup granulated sugar**
⅓ **cup water**
1 **tablespoon corn syrup**
⅛ **teaspoon salt**
2 **egg whites**
1 **teaspoon vanilla extract**

1. Combine all ingredients except vanilla extract, and mix well in top of a double boiler. Place over simmering water and immediately beat with rotary beater for 7 to 10 minutes, or until mixture holds stiff peaks.
2. Remove from water and blend in vanilla extract. Beat until cool and thick enough to spread.

About 5½ cups frosting

The following cake can be baked using either a marbled effect or a "gob" effect, chocolate and white spoonfuls of batter dropped in the pan alternately. The hot, baked cake is then topped with marshmallows which melt and adhere as it cools. Then the marshmallows are covered with a chocolate icing.

This cake, a favorite of sweets eaters of all ages, will travel well if returned to the pan when frosted.

Marble or Gob Cake

1½ **ounces (1½ squares)**
 unsweetened chocolate
½ **cup butter**
2 **teaspoons vanilla extract**
1 **cup sugar**
2 **cups sifted cake flour**
2 **teaspoons baking powder**
½ **teaspoon salt**
¾ **cup milk**
3 **egg whites**
2 **tablespoons hot water**
1 **tablespoon sugar**
½ **teaspoon baking soda**
18 **marshmallows, halved**
 Chocolate Icing

1. Melt chocolate over hot water.
2. Meanwhile, cream butter with vanilla extract in bowl of electric mixer. Add 1 cup sugar gradually, creaming until fluffy.
3. Sift flour with baking powder and salt. Add dry ingredients to batter in fourths, alternating with milk in thirds, beating until smooth after each addition.
4. Beat egg whites until stiff, but not dry. Spread batter over egg whites and carefully fold together.
5. Grease an 8-inch springform pan and line bottom with greased parchment paper.
6. Decide whether you want a marbled or a "gob" effect and follow either step 7 or 8 accordingly.
7. *For marbled effect:* Turn 2½ cups of batter into pan. Mix melted chocolate with hot water, 1 tablespoon sugar, and baking soda. Gently blend with

Step 10

remaining batter. Drop spoonfuls of chocolate mixture over top of white batter. Then gently lift white batter through chocolate batter to produce marbled effect, being *very careful* not to over-blend.

8. *For gob effect:* Put 2½ cups of batter into another bowl. Mix melted chocolate with hot water, 1 tablespoon sugar, and baking soda. Gently blend with smaller portion of batter. Drop alternating gobs of white and chocolate batters into the pan. Add second layer in the same alternating fashion, this time putting chocolate over white. Repeat, putting white over chocolate, chocolate over white, until all batter has been used.

9. Bake at 350°F about 40 minutes, or until cake tests done. Remove side of springform and invert cake on rack; then remove pan bottom and peel off parchment paper. Invert cake so that it is right side up on rack.

10. Return side of springform to cake; this will act as a fence around cake so that marshmallows will not slip off as they melt. Place marshmallow halves, sticky side down, on top of cake to cover completely. Set aside to cool; the heat from the cooling cake will melt the marshmallows.

11. When cool, use a knife blade to loosen marshmallows stuck to pan. Remove pan side. Cover marshmallows completely with Chocolate Icing, using spatula.

One 8-inch cake

Chocolate Icing

2 ounces (2 squares) unsweetened chocolate
1 egg white
1 cup confectioners' sugar
Water (1 or 2 tablespoons)

1. Melt chocolate over hot water. When melted, scrape into small bowl of electric mixer. Add egg white, confectioners' sugar, and 1 tablespoon water. Beat well.

2. When icing is mixed, check consistency; it should be thin enough to spread easily, but not so thin that it runs immediately off of spoon. You may have to add 1 more tablespoon water. Mix until well combined.

About 1 cup icing

Dobos Torte
Torte Layers

Caramel Topping:
¾ cup sugar
Chocolate Buttercream
½ cup finely chopped walnuts

1. Prepare Torte Layers. When they are cool, choose the flattest and most perfect one and lay it in the center of a large sheet of waxed paper. Butter a large knife and lay it to the side of the waxed paper along with a spatula.

2. For Caramel Topping, put sugar into a heavy, light-colored skillet and set over low heat. Stir

Step 3

constantly with a wooden spoon until sugar lique-fies. Continue stirring until liquid turns a golden brown.

3. Pour syrup over torte layer on waxed paper, and use spatula to work syrup out to edges of layer. Spread quickly as caramel hardens in a short time.

4. With a buttered knife, cut caramelized layer into 8 equal wedges.

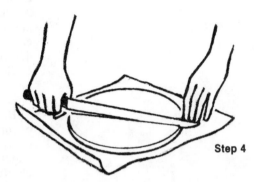

Step 4

5. To assemble torte, place 1 torte layer on serving plate and cover with ⅓ cup Chocolate Butter-cream. Lay second layer on top of first and cover with same amount of buttercream. Repeat, layer-ing and frosting until 7 layers are covered with frosting.

6. Frost sides of torte and press chopped nuts into frosting around sides. Arrange caramel-covered wedges in a circle on top of cake and spoon a dab of buttercream under each wedge to prop it up

Step 5

Step 6

(see illustration). Then pipe a rosette in center of cake top. Refrigerate until serving time. Serve slightly chilled. Cake will taste better if allowed to ripen in refrigerator for 12 hours before serving and will keep for several days in the refrigerator.

One 8-inch torte

Torte Layers

6 egg yolks
³/₄ cup sugar
1 cup all-purpose flour
¹/₈ teaspoon baking powder
¹/₈ teaspoon salt
3 tablespoons water
6 egg whites

1. Cut eight 8-inch circles from parchment paper, and set them on cookie sheets—as many as will fit into your oven. (Or, if desired, place parchment paper circles on inverted layer cake pans.) Grease and flour parchment paper circles well.
2. Beat egg yolks with sugar in large bowl of electric mixer until thick. Add flour, baking powder, and salt and beat again. Then add water and mix until well combined.
3. Meanwhile, beat whites until stiff, but not dry, and fold them into batter (there should be about 5 cups).
4. Ladle a scant cup batter onto each prepared circle; use spatula to spread batter as evenly as possible. (Don't worry if spread batter looks thin or holey; this will bake out to some extent.)
5. Bake at 300°F 10 to 12 minutes, or until edges become crisp and golden. Remove layers from oven and slide them, still attached to parchment paper, onto wire racks. When slightly cooled, carefully peel off paper.
6. Meanwhile, grease and flour the second batch of parchment paper circles and cover them with batter. As soon as first batch comes out of the oven, place second batch on cookie sheets and bake. Repeat with remaining batter until all is used. You will have 8 layers.

8 torte layers

Chocolate Buttercream

1 cup (6 ounces) semisweet
   chocolate pieces
½ ounce (½ square) unsweetened
   chocolate
1½ cups unsalted butter
1¼ cups sugar
2 egg yolks
2 tablespoons rum (or 1 teaspoon
   rum extract)
¹/₈ teaspoon salt

1. Melt chocolate pieces and unsweetened chocolate in top of a double boiler. Cool over cold water.
2. Beat butter in large bowl of electric mixer until fluffy. Add sugar gradually, beating thoroughly to incorporate, and then add egg yolks, rum, and salt. Beat in cooled chocolate.
3. If necessary, refrigerate soft, freshly made frosting until of proper consistency to spread. Buttercream frosting will keep for several days in a covered container in the refrigerator.

About 4 cups buttercream

Chocolate Dobos Torte
Chocolate Torte Layers

Chocolate Topping:
1¼ cups semisweet chocolate pieces
¹/₃ cup butter
   Coffee Buttercream
½ cup finely chopped walnuts

1. Prepare Chocolate Torte Layers.
2. While layers cool, make Chocolate Topping. Lay remaining 8-inch parchment paper circle in an ungreased 8-inch layer cake pan.
3. Melt semisweet chocolate pieces in top of a double boiler, and when melted, add butter and

stir until butter is melted and well combined. Turn chocolate into pan and, with spatula, spread as evenly as possible. Refrigerate until hardened.

4. To assemble torte, place 1 torte layer on a serving plate (see Note). Cover with ⅓ cup Coffee Buttercream. Lay second layer on top of first and cover with same amount of buttercream. Repeat, layering and frosting until all 8 layers are covered with frosting. Use half of remaining buttercream to frost sides. Press walnuts into frosting on sides of cake.

5. Remove cake pan from refrigerator and run a knife blade carefully around sides of hardened chocolate. Turn chocolate layer out onto top of cake. With a long, sharp knife, score chocolate into 8 equal wedges.

6. Using a pastry bag and large star tube, fill with remaining buttercream frosting and pipe a border around base of cake.

7. Refrigerate until serving time and serve slightly chilled. Cake will taste better if allowed to ripen in refrigerator for 12 hours before serving and will keep for several days in the refrigerator.

One 8-inch torte

Note: Dobos layers, made to be crips, will stiffen out of shape and become brittle as they cool. During assembly, flatten each between your hands, allowing the layers to break into pieces when necessary. Frost as usual, piecing layers as needed. Buttercream will hold everything together.

Chocolate Torte Layers

6 egg yolks
1¼ cups sugar
⅔ cup sifted cake flour
½ teaspoon baking powder
¼ teaspoon baking soda
⅓ cup rum
4 ounces (4 squares) unsweetened chocolate
6 egg whites

1. Cut nine 8-inch circles from parchment paper; grease and flour 8 of them and lay these on ungreased cookie sheets. Reserve remaining circle for chocolate topping.

2. Beat yolks with sugar in large bowl of electric mixer until thick. Add flour, baking powder, and baking soda and mix well. Then add rum and mix again.

3. Meanwhile, melt chocolate over hot water. Cool slightly and add to mixture. Then beat egg whites until stiff. Fold batter into egg whites. There will be about 3½ cups batter.

4. Ladle a scant ½ cup batter onto each prepared paper circle, using spatula to spread batter.

5. Bake at 350°F 12 to 14 minutes, or until they test done. Layers may have to be baked in two batches.

6. Remove layers from oven and slide them, still attached to paper, onto wire racks. When cooled slightly, carefully peel off paper.

8 torte layers

Coffee Buttercream

6 egg yolks
1 cup sugar
⅔ cup hot milk
2½ tablespoons freeze-dried coffee
2 cups chilled unsalted butter, cut
   in pieces

1. Put egg yolks and sugar into a bowl and beat until thick. Add hot milk gradually, beating constantly. Pour into a heavy saucepan. Cook, stirring continuously, about 7 minutes, or until thickened.

2. Remove from heat, add coffee, and stir until dissolved. Pour into a bowl and beat 1 minute to cool slightly. Add butter, a small amount at a time, beating after each addition until butter is melted.

About 4½ cups buttercream

Note: If desired, chill frosting, then beat until smooth before using.

Simple Outside
Decorated Cakes

All frosting is ornamental, as we said in the Introduction; spreading the simplest uncooked icing over a pan of brownies is a way of decorating them. This chapter contains a number of cakes, each covered with some kind of easy-to-apply, outside decoration. These range from the simplest design, made by sifting confectioners' sugar over a doily set on a cake top, to a chocolate cake baked in the shape of a lamb, frosted with a delicious cooked choclate frosting, and covered with chocolate-coated corn flake crumbs.

The hardest thing you'll be asked to do in this chapter, then, is to frost a cake—a relatively simple task once a few of the following steps are learned.

●

TO FROST A CAKE

1. Lay four thin strips of waxed paper on a serving platter (see illustration). (If you wish the cake to

sit on a doily, put the doily on the platter first; then cover with paper strips.) The waxed paper will protect the serving platter from the inevitable drip that accompanies a cake being decorated.

Note: If you wish to frost the cake on a separate plate and then transfer it to the serving platter, cut circles just slightly smaller than the cake out of corrugated cardboard, cover with aluminum foil, and place them under the layers before frosting; then use these to transfer cake to serving platter.

2. Set the first layer on the waxed paper, right side up, then brush excess crumbs off of layer with fingers. With a decorator's spatula (see illustration), cover top of layer generously with icing, spreading it out evenly to edges.

3. Brush crumbs off of second layer and invert it over first layer. The bottom surface of the cake layer should now be the top of the cake (see illustration).

4. Spread a very thin layer of icing over the top and sides of cake. This icing undercoat will stabilize the crumbs. Let the cake sit for several moments to allow the undercoat to set.

Note: Some decorators prefer to undercoat a cake with a jam glaze, rather than use the thin layer of icing. If used correctly, this can add a faint, elusive, extra taste to the cake. To make glaze:

(a) Choose a complementary taste; apricot is the most popular, but lemon curd, raspberry, or even orange marmalade is effective on the right cake.

(b) Sieve enough jam to yield about 1 cup and heat for a moment, stirring constantly, until warm to the touch.

(c) Use a pastry brush to apply warm jam to top and sides of cake. (Cake should be filled and layered beforehand.) Then refrigerate for a few moments until jam cools and sets, before covering with icing as directed.

5. To frost the cake, use a spatula to cover the sides with icing first, making upward strokes from bottom to top. Then cover the top. Spoon icing onto the center of top layer and spread to edge with spatula. Examine cake on all sides to be sure it's completely covered with icing.

6. For a smooth finish, have a deep pot full of boiling water near the cake. Dip the spatula into it frequently while smoothing top and sides, making them as level as possible. If you wish to make decorative patterns in icing or to add further ornaments, see To Decorate A Frosted Cake (page 29).

7. Let the icing set; then gently pull the waxed paper strips out from under cake, one at a time. The cake can be left at room temperature if you're planning on serving it within a few hours; otherwise, place it in the refrigerator, being careful not to set it near anything strong smelling such as onions, spicy leftovers, or strong-smelling cheeses, since cakes absorb odors easily.

8. When icing sets, cover cake, if desired, with a foil

nt; that is, enclose cake in a sheet of foil that is uffed out at sides and fastened high enough above op of cake so that icing isn't touched.

O DECORATE A FROSTED CAKE

Many things can be done to a frosted cake to make interesting, including swirling the icing or pressing nuts into the sides. The few ideas below are intended merely to be used as departure points for your own creativity. Remember, though, that any ecoration added to icing should have integrity—a urpose for its being there beyond ornamentation. Choose decorations that reflect a color, a flavor, an ingredient, or the theme of the cake. And, qually important, make sure that the cake, icing, and decoration will taste good together.

To peak icing: Pile icing thickly onto top and sides f cake. Use a rubber spatula or back of a large ablespoon to make peaks. Press tool down lightly into soft icing; then remove tool by pulling t straight up. Icing will form soft peaks (see illustration).

To swirl icing: Pile icing thickly onto top and sides f cake. With back tip of a large tablespoon, make soft indentations in icing, one after another in ows (see illustration).

To hobnail icing: Cover top and sides of cake thickly with icing. Press back of spoon into icing to leave rounded indentations. Do this at regular intervals, making hobnails next to each other (see illustration).

To decorate a chocolate cake frosted with white icing: Melt 2 ounces dark sweet chocolate along with a scant teaspoon of butter; mix well and dribble it around sides (see illustration).

To decorate a white cake frosted with white icing and filled with chocolate filling: Allow icing to set; then melt dark sweet or semisweet chocolate and use a pastry brush to cover icing completely with chocolate (see illustration).

To use a decorating comb: Trail one side of this triangular-shaped tool over still-soft icing surface to make waves, ridges, or scallops (see illustration).

To make a cake that resembles a porcupine, a portion of this cake is baked in a 2½-quart oven-proof bowl. The layers are spread with almond filling and the cake covered with almond frosting studded with slivered almonds. Children love both to add the "quills" and eat the cake.

Almond Porcupine Cake

3³/₄ cups sifted cake flour
1½ tablespoons baking powder
³/₄ teaspoon salt
1 cup butter
1½ teaspoons vanilla extract
³/₄ teaspoon almond extract
1³/₄ cups sugar
10 egg yolks
1¼ cups milk
Almond Filling
Almond Frosting
¼ cup slivered blanched almonds

1. Grease a 9-inch round layer cake pan and dust with flour. Grease a 2½ quart oven-proof mixing bowl (8 to 9 inches in diameter) and dust with flour. Set pan and bowl aside.
2. Sift flour with baking powder and salt. Set aside.
3. Cream butter with extracts and sugar until mixture is like whipped cream. Add egg yolks, one at a time, beating thoroughly after each addition, then beat 5 minutes.
4. Add dry ingredients alternately with milk in thirds, beating well after each addition. Pour 4½ cups batter into the prepared bowl and the remaining batter into the cake pan.
5. Bake at 300°F 30 to 35 minutes for the layer in the cake pan, and about 1 hour and 25 minutes for the cake in the bowl, or until cakes test done.
6. Set pan and bowl on wire racks to cool 10 minutes. Turn layer out of pan onto wire rack. If necessary, loosen sides of cake from bowl with a knife before turning out. Cool both cakes completely.
7. When cool, place the 9-inch cake layer on a serving plate and spread with ½ cup Almond Filling.
8. Divide cake baked in bowl horizontally into 3 layers of even depth, using a long-bladed, serrated knife. Place the largest layer on the 9-inch layer. Spread with ½ cup filling. Put second layer in place, spread with remaining filling, and top with third layer. (Cake should resemble an inverted bowl.)
9. Cover outside of cake with Almond Frosting, using a spatula to smooth the frosting as much as possible. Stick almonds at random in frosting.

One 4-layer 9-inch cake

Almond Filling

¼ cup butter, softened
1 can (8 ounces) almond paste, cut in pieces
¼ cup milk

Combine butter and almond paste in a medium bowl. Beat until well mixed, soft, and creamy; add milk and beat until mixture is creamy enough to spread easily. Refrigerate, if not to be used immediately. If refrigerated, beat again until soft enough to spread before using.

1¼ cups filling

Almond Frosting

1 **cup sugar**
6 **tablespoons water**
¼ **teaspoon cream of tartar**
2 **egg whites**
⅛ **teaspoon salt**
1½ **teaspoons almond extract**
¾ **teaspoon vanilla extract**

1. Combine sugar, water, and cream of tartar in a small, heavy saucepan. Stir over low heat until sugar is dissolved. Cover saucepan and bring mixture to boiling; boil gently 5 minutes. Uncover and put candy thermometer in place. During cooking, wash sugar crystals from sides of pan with a pastry brush dipped in water. Cook without stirring until mixture reaches 244°F (firm-ball stage).
2. Meanwhile, beat egg whites with electric mixer until peaks are stiff, but not dry. Beating continuously, pour hot syrup over beaten egg whites in a thin, steady stream (do not scrape pan).
3. After all the hot syrup has been added, add salt and extracts. Continue beating 2 to 3 minutes, or until frosting forms rounded peaks and holds its shape. Use immediately.

2 cups frosting

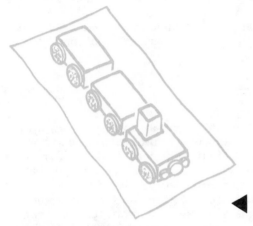

A cake in the shape of a favorite toy often delights children. For railroad enthusiasts, a square cake can be cut into pieces which are frosted, arranged, and decorated to resemble the cars of a freight train. So simple to make, this cake is a treat for mothers as well as children.

Train Cake

Three-Egg Cake, chilled
Browned Butter Frosting (see
Note)
12 **round, flat cookies or candies, 1**
to 2 inches in diameter, to be
used for wheels (sandwich
cookies, party mints, red-hot
dollars, or lollipops with
sticks removed may be used)
3 **licorice sticks, halved**
1 **large marshmallow half (cut**
crosswise)
2 **red gumdrops**

1. Invert the cake so it is bottom side up. Cut 3 pieces of cake 5×3½ inches each, and cut 1 piece 3×1½ inches for smoke stack.
2. Cover the top and sides of the pieces with Browned Butter Frosting, spreading as smoothly as possible with a metal spatula dipped frequently in hot water. Place smoke stack on one car of train to make engine.
3. Arrange cars to form a train on a serving platter.
4. Immediately, before frosting begins to set, press or prop round cookies in place on both sides of cars to form wheels. Connect wheels with licorice sticks for "axles." Press sticky side of marshmallow half on front of first car, making a headlight. Place a gumdrop on each side of marshmallow.
5. Using a large pastry bag, filled with frosting, and tube 4 (plain), pipe a border around the edge of train and smoke stack (see photo).

One 3-car train cake

Note: If desired, Train Cake may be covered with chocolate icing. Sieve enough raspberry or apricot jam to make ⅔ cup. Spread each piece of cake with sieved jam and chill thoroughly. Make Poured Chocolate Icing (page 73) and pour over pieces of cake placed on wire racks, coating cake thoroughly.

Three-Egg Cake

¾ **cup butter**
1 **cup sugar**
⅔ **cup firmly packed brown sugar**
3 **eggs**
2¾ **cups sifted cake flour**
2¾ **teaspoons baking powder**
¼ **teaspoon salt**
1 **cup milk**
1½ **teaspoons vanilla extract**

1. Cream butter until fluffy in large bowl of an electric mixer. Add sugars, beating until well combined. Add eggs, one at a time, beating well after each addition.
2. Sift flour with baking powder and salt. Add to batter in fourths alternately with milk and vanilla extract, beginning and ending with flour. When thoroughly combined, spoon into a well-greased 9-inch square baking pan that has been lined on the bottom with greased parchment paper. Smooth top with a spatula, pushing batter into the corners.
3. Bake at 350°F 40 minutes, or until cake tests done. Turn out on wire rack and cool completely. Peel off paper.

Browned Butter Frosting

½ **cup butter**
4 **cups confectioners' sugar**
½ **cup half-and-half (more if needed)**
1 **tablespoon dark corn syrup**
1 **teaspoon vanilla extract**

1. Melt butter in a heavy saucepan over low heat. Continue heating until it turns deep golden brown, watching carefully so it does not burn. Remove from heat and stir in confectioners' sugar, half-and-half, corn syrup, and vanilla extract.
2. Beat well, using an electric mixer or wire whisk. Frosting must be creamy and soft, yet stiff enough to spread on cake. Beat in additional confectioners' sugar or half-and-half as needed to reach desired consistency.

Old-fashioned Chocolate Cake

1½ **ounces (1½ squares)
   unsweetened chocolate**
6 **tablespoons butter**
¾ **teaspoon vanilla extract**
1½ **cups firmly packed dark brown
   sugar**
2 **egg yolks**
1⅔ **cups sifted all-purpose flour**
3 **tablespoons cocoa**
¾ **teaspoon baking powder**
¾ **teaspoon baking soda**
¼ **teaspoon salt**
⅓ **cup milk**
2 **teaspoons fresh lemon juice**
¾ **cup warm water**
2 **egg whites**
1 **to 2 tablespoons confectioners'
   sugar**

1. Melt chocolate over hot water. Cool.
2. Cream butter with vanilla extract in bowl of electric mixer. Add brown sugar gradually, mixing well. Add egg yolks, beat until blended, and stir in cooled chocolate.
3. Sift flour with cocoa, baking powder, baking soda, and salt. Set aside.
4. Pour milk and lemon juice into a small bowl and let stand until milk curdles. Stir in water.
5. Add dry ingredients to batter in 4 portions alternately with milk mixture, beating constantly.
6. Beat egg whites until peaks are stiff, but not dry; fold batter into egg whites. Pour into a well-greased and floured 10-inch glass pie plate.
7. Bake at 300°F 55 to 60 minutes. Remove from oven, loosen from plate, immediately turn out onto a wire rack, and turn right side up. Wash and dry pie plate.
8. When cake is cool, return to pie plate. Just before serving, lay a 10-inch round lace paper doily on top of cake and sift confectioners' sugar over top. Carefully remove doily.

9. The cake may be served immediately, or kept covered in refrigerator for several days.

One 10-inch cake

NOTE: To make your own doily, cut a stiff piece of paper into a circle the diameter of the cake. Fold it in half, then twice again. Draw several small decorative shapes on top surface of folded paper. Cut out these shapes with a sharp scissors and unfold paper to see pattern repeat.

The following three cakes all have cooked-on cake toppings. The spice cake has a meringue that is swirled onto the batter, sprinkled with nuts, and baked with the cake. The upside-down cake has a fruit decoration that shows up only when the cake is inverted and the pan removed. The lemon cake has an attractive topping that is spread on a fully baked cake and broiled until bubbly.

Apple Upside-down Cake

Topping:

   3 **large baking apples (about 1 pound)**
   2 **tablespoons lemon juice**
 1/2 **cup water**
 1/3 **cup butter or margarine**
 3/4 **cup firmly packed light brown sugar**
 1/8 **teaspoonspoon cinnamon**
   2 **teaspoons finely grated lemon peel**
 10 **candied cherries**

Cake batter:

1¾ **cups sifted cake flour**
   1 **teaspoon baking powder**
 1/2 **teaspoon salt**
   3 **egg yolks**
 1/2 **cup sugar**
 1/3 **cup orange juice**
   2 **tablespoons lemon juice**
   3 **egg whites**
 1/2 **cup sugar**
    Sweetened whipped cream, optional

1. For topping, pare, core, and slice apples into ten 1/2-inch thick rings. Combine lemon juice with water and dip apple rings in the water to prevent browning.

2. Melt butter in a heavy 10-inch skillet (2 inches deep) with a heat-resistant handle. Blend in brown sugar, salt, cinnamon, and lemon peel. Arrange apple rings in syrup, placing cherries in center of each ring.

3. For cake batter, sift the flour with baking powder and salt; set aside.

4. Beat egg yolks until thick and lemon colored. Gradually add 1/2 cup sugar and orange fruit juice, beating thoroughly. Sift dry ingredients about one fourth at a time over egg yolk mixture and gently fold until just blended after each addition. Set aside.

5. Beat egg whites until frothy. Gradually add 1/2 cup sugar, continuing to beat until stiff peaks are formed. Gently fold batter into meringue until just blended. Turn batter into skillet over apple rings, spreading evenly.

6. Bake at 350°F 40 to 50 minutes, or until cake tests done.

7. Using a spatula, loosen cake from sides of skillet and immediately invert onto a serving plate. Allow skillet to remain over cake a few seconds so syrup will drain onto cake. Remove skillet.

8. Serve cake warm, topping each wedge with a spoonful of sweetened whipped cream, if desired.

One 10-inch cake

Blueberry Upside-down Cake: Follow recipe for Apple Upside-down Cake. For topping, substitute **½ cup granulated sugar** for the brown sugar, omit cinnamon and lemon peel, and substitute **2 cups fresh blueberries** for the apples and cherries.

Peach Upside-down Cake: Follow recipe for Apple Upside-down Cake. For topping, reduce brown sugar to ½ cup, omit cinnamon and lemon peel, and substitute **4 medium (about 1 pound) firm ripe peaches,** peeled and sliced, for the apples and cherries.

Apple Spice Cake with Meringue

- ⅓ **cup butter**
- 1 **teaspoon vanilla extract**
- ⅔ **cup firmly packed brown sugar**
- 1 **egg**
- 1 **egg yolk**
- 1½ **cups sifted cake flour**
- ¾ **teaspoon baking powder**
- ¾ **teaspoon baking soda**
- ½ **teaspoon cinnamon**
- ⅛ **teaspoon each salt, allspice, and nutmeg**
- 3 **tablespoons milk**
- ½ **cup dairy sour cream**
- 1½ **cups chopped pared apple**
- 4 **egg whites**
- 1 **cup granulated sugar**
- ⅛ **teaspoon salt**
- ½ **cup chopped walnuts**

1. Cream butter with vanilla extract in large bowl of electric mixer. Add brown sugar and mix well. Add egg and egg yolk; mix well.
2. Combine flour with baking powder, baking soda, cinnamon, salt, allspice, and nutmeg. Add dry ingredients to creamed mixture alternately with milk and sour cream, mixing well after each addition.
3. Stir in chopped apple; mix well. Spoon batter into a well-greased 13×9-inch baking pan, spreading evenly with a spatula.
4. Beat egg whites, using an electric mixer, until they hold soft peaks. Beating continuously, add sugar and salt gradually. Continue to beat 1 minute after sugar has been added.
5. Spoon the meringue over cake batter around edge. Using a spatula, gently spread meringue toward the center, leaving a space 1½ inches in diameter in center of cake. Sprinkle walnuts over meringue.
6. Bake at 325°F about 45 minutes, or until cake tests done.
7. Set pan on a wire rack and allow cake to cool in pan.

One 13×9 inch cake

White Sheet Cake with Broiler Icing

White Sheet Cake:
- 1 **cup butter**
- 2 **cups sugar**
- 3¼ **cups sifted cake flour**
- 1 **tablespoon baking powder**
- ⅛ **teaspoon salt**
- 1 **cup milk**
- 1½ **teaspoons lemon extract**
- 6 **egg whites**
- ⅛ **teaspoon cream of tartar**

1. For cake, grease a 15×10×1-inch jelly-roll pan. Line bottom with parchment paper and grease paper. Set pan aside.
2. Cream butter with sugar in large bowl of electric mixer. Mix flour with baking powder and salt; add to creamed mixture alternately with milk. Beat in lemon extract.
3. Beat egg whites and cream of tartar until peaks are stiff, but not dry. Spoon batter over egg whites and fold together, allowing a few unmixed por-

Lemon Broiler Icing:
- **7** tablespoons butter
- **1⅔** cups firmly packed light brown sugar
- **¼** teaspoon salt
- **1½** teaspoons grated lemon peel
- **¼** cup strained fresh lemon juice
- **1¼** cups flaked coconut or crushed shredded wheat cereal

tions to remain. Spoon batter into the prepared jelly-roll pan; spread evenly from center to sides.

4. Bake at 350°F about 30 minutes, or until cake tests done. Immediately turn cake out onto wire rack to cool 30 minutes. Peel off paper.

5. For icing, in a small bowl, cream butter with brown sugar. Add salt, lemon peel, and lemon juice; mix well. Stir in coconut, combining thoroughly.

6. Return cake to baking pan and spread top with icing.

7. Place cake under broiler so top is about 4 inches from heat. Broil about 2 minutes, or until icing bubbles. Watch closely to avoid scorching. Since pan is large, corners sometimes do not heat as fast as center. If desired, hold pan under broiler for an additional minute or so, to heat corners.

One 15×10-inch cake

This lamb cake is perfect for an Easter centerpiece and is a delight for children. Baked in a two-piece lamb mold, the cake is made using a cake mix or a favorite layer-cake recipe. The lamb is placed on a rectangular cake base and is decorated according to the flavor of the cake.

Lamb Cake

- **2** packages (about 18 ounces each) cake mix
- Frosting and coating for lamb cake (see below)
- **2** golden raisins
- **1** candied red cherry half

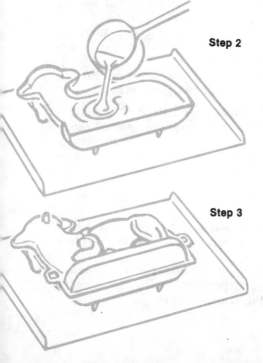

Step 2

Step 3

1. Liberally grease the inside of a 2-piece lamb mold, being sure to grease the ears well. Sprinkle lightly with flour and lay front half of mold on a baking sheet. Grease and flour a 13×9-inch baking pan. Set both pans aside.

2. Prepare batter for 1 cake according to package directions. Pour batter into mold-on-baking sheet, filling it level, being sure ears are filled with batter. Lay half a wooden pick in each ear for added strength. Place back half of lamb mold on face half. Tie cord around the mold to hold in place.

3. Prepare batter for other cake, following package directions. Pour into prepared rectangular pan. Bake both cakes, following temperature and timing for rectangular cake according to package directions. Lamb cake may require a few more minutes of baking than the other cake. Test it by inserting a wooden pick through hole in back side of mold, remove back half of mold and check for doneness with a wooden pick.

4. Turn rectangular cake out onto a wire rack immediately to cool. Leave lamb-shaped cake in mold about 3 minutes before opening. Remove back half only and let cake rest standing up in front half of mold about 1 hour. Remove from mold and gently lay on wire rack, nose side up, until cool.

(cont.)

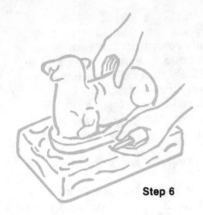

Step 6

Spice Lamb Cake

5. If rectangular cake is rounded in center, slice off excess and save. Place cooled rectangular cake, bottom side up, on a large serving platter. Using a spatula, cover top and sides with frosting, spreading as smoothly as possible.

6. Set lamb cake on the frosted cake, slightly off center and toward the back. If lamb does not sit level, prop it up, using trimmed cake pieces. Cover lamb carefully and smoothly with seven-minute frosting, using a knife to apply frosting on face and ears.

7. Press an ample amount of cereal coating over the entire body, neck, and head of lamb, running a small amount down center of nose. Do not cover face or front of ears with topping. Press raisins in place for eyes and cherry half for nose. If any coating remains sprinkle it on bottom cake around lamb.

1 lamb cake with base

White Lamb Cake: Follow recipe for Lamb Cake using **white cake mixes, Seven-Minute Frosting,** and **2 cups flaked coconut** for coating.

Chocolate Lamb Cake: Follow recipe for Lamb Cake using **chocolate cake mixes, Chocolate Seven-Minute Frosting,** and **Chocolate Cereal Coating.**

Spice Lamb Cake: Follow recipe for Lamb Cake using **spice cake mixes, Brown Sugar Seven-Minute Frosting** (page 21; use 1½ times recipe), and **2 cups chopped walnuts** for coating.

Seven-Minute Frosting

2¼ **cups granulated sugar**
 ½ **cup water**
1½ **tablespoons light corn syrup**
 ¼ **teaspoon salt**
 3 **egg whites**
1½ **teaspoons vanilla extract**

1. Combine sugar, water, corn syrup, salt, and egg whites in the top of a double boiler; mix well.
2. Place over simmering water and immediately beat with a rotary beater 7 to 10 minutes, or until mixture holds peaks.
3. Remove from heat and blend in vanilla extract. Beat until cool and thick enough to spread.

Chocolate Seven-Minute Frosting:
Melt **4½ ounces (4½ squares) unsweetened chocolate;** set aside to cool. Follow recipe for Seven-Minute Frosting. Blend in cooled chocolate along with the vanilla extract.

Chocolate Cereal Coating

 1 **package (6 ounces) semisweet chocolate pieces**
 3 **tablespoons butter**
 2 **cups corn flakes**

1. Melt chocolate and butter in top of a double boiler; stir to mix well. Add corn flakes and toss gently.
2. Lay coated cereal on waxed paper, separating flakes as much as possible. Refrigerate about 5 .minutes, or until no longer sticky.

Dried figs add a new dimension to this traditional fruitcake. It can be decorated soon after it is baked, or it can be wrapped and refrigerated to age several months before it is decorated. For a different serving idea, make the miniature fruitcakes.

Decorated Fruitcake

Fruitcake:
1½ cups (about 9 ounces) snipped dried figs
1 cup (about 6 ounces) snipped pitted dates
1 cup (about 5 ounces) dark seedless raisins
1 cup (about 5 ounces) golden raisins
1 cup (about 5 ounces) diced candied citron
1 cup (about 5 ounces) diced candied lemon peel
1 cup (about 5 ounces) diced candied orange peel
½ cup (about 3 ounces) diced candied pineapple
½ cup (about 3 ounces) halved red candied cherries
½ cup (about 2 ounces) currants
½ cup apricot brandy
½ cup orange juice
1 cup (4 ounces) blanched almond halves
4 cups sifted all-purpose flour
2 teaspoons baking powder
½ teaspoon salt
1 teaspoon ground cinnamon
½ teaspoon ground nutmeg
1 cup butter
1 teaspoon orange extract
2 cups sugar
6 eggs

Glaze:
⅓ cup sugar
½ cup water
½ cup dark corn syrup
Candied cherry halves
Whole almonds, blanched and split lengthwise

1. For fruitcake, combine fruits, brandy, and orange juice in a large bowl. (If desired, use either all brandy or all orange juice.) Cover tightly and set aside for 24 hours; stir occasionally.
2. Grease bottom and sides of a 10-inch tube pan. Line bottom and sides with greased parchment paper; set aside.
3. Add nuts to fruit. Sift flour with baking powder, salt, cinnamon, and nutmeg over fruit and nuts; toss until pieces are well coated.
4. Cream butter with orange extract and sugar in a large bowl; beat until light and fluffy. Add eggs, one at a time, beating thoroughly after each addition. (Mixture may be slightly curdled, but this will not affect the final product.) Using a spoon, thoroughly combine the creamed and fruit-nut mixtures. Spoon batter into prepared pan; spread evenly.
5. Bake at 300°F 2 hours and 40 minutes, or until cake tests done. Cool completely on wire rack before removing from pan. If desired, spoon ¼ cup apricot brandy or orange juice over cake as soon as it has finished baking.
6. When cool, remove from pan and peel off paper. If not to be served immediately, wrap and store in refrigerator.
7. Prepare Glaze when cake is cool and ready to serve. Combine sugar, water, and corn syrup in a small saucepan. Bring to boiling and boil for 2 minutes. Remove from heat and immediately brush on cake.
8. Arrange fruit and nuts on top of cake to form flowers. Use 5 almonds to form petals and a cherry half for center of each flower (see photo). Or decorate as desired. Immediately brush completed decorations with remaining glaze, and set aside to dry.
9. Wrap and refrigerate when glaze is dry. Slicing is easier when cake is cold.

6¾ pounds fruitcake

Miniature fruitcakes: Follow recipe for Decorated Fruitcake; spoon batter into muffin pans. Bake at 300 °F 45 minutes. Decorate cake with one flower, then glaze as above.

This delicious cake is not only beautiful to look at, but quite simple to make. The cake is filled and frosted with Lemon Curd Buttercream, covered with Italian Meringue, and browned in the oven.

Lemon Meringue Cake

4 **egg yolks**
½ **cup sugar**
¼ **cup water**
1 **teaspoon lemon extract**
1 **cup sifted cake flour**
4 **egg whites**
½ **teaspoon cream of tartar**
⅛ **teaspoon salt**
½ **cup sugar**
Lemon Curd Buttercream
Italian Meringue

1. Grease bottom and sides of a 15x10x1-inch jelly-roll pan. Line bottom with parchment paper and grease the paper. Set aside.
2. In large bowl of an electric mixer, beat the egg yolks with ½ cup sugar, water, and lemon extract until very thick. Stir in flour until just blended.
3. Beat egg whites with cream of tartar and salt until soft peaks are formed. Gradually add ½ cup sugar, continuing to beat until stiff peaks are formed. Fold egg yolk mixture into meringue until blended. Turn batter into prepared pan and spread evenly.
4. Bake at 350°F 20 to 25 minutes, or until cake tests done. Turn out onto wire rack to cool. Peel off paper.
5. When cake is cool, cut into two 10x7½ inch pieces, forming 2 layers. Place 1 layer on an oven-proof serving plate.
6. Beat Lemon Curd Buttercream to soften, if necessary. Spread ⅔ cup over top of bottom layer. Place second layer on top. Cover top and sides of cake with remaining buttercream. Refrigerate until chilled (about 30 minutes).
7. Using a large pastry bag and tube 6 or 7 (plain), fill (page 39) with Italian Meringue. Cover top and sides of chilled cake with meringue snails (see illustration).
8. Bake at 400°F 5 to 8 minutes (oven must be preheated), or until meringue peaks are lightly browned. Remove from oven and chill immediately. Serve cold.

One 10x7-inch layer cake

Note: This cake may be made as a single layer. Do not cut cake in half. Cover top and sides with frosting and make a double recipe of meringue to cover chilled cake.

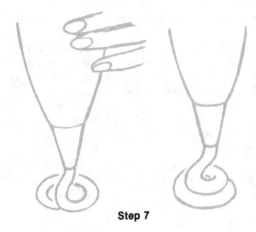

Step 7

Lemon Curd Buttercream

¼ **cup butter**
5 **egg yolks**
1 **cup sugar**
1 **tablespoon grated lemon peel**
5 **tablespoons strained fresh lemon juice**
½ **cup butter**

1. Combine ¼ cup butter, egg yolks, sugar, lemon peel, and juice in top of a double boiler. Cook over boiling water, stirring slowly but steadily with a wooden spoon until it is slightly thicker (about 10 minutes). Continue cooking over boiling water, stirring occasionally, until curd becomes thick (about 20 minutes). Add more boiling water to

double boiler as necessary. Remove from heat and cool.

2. Beat ½ cup butter in a mixing bowl, using an electric mixer, until fluffy. Beating constantly, add cooled lemon mixture, ¼ cup at a time, beating until all has been added and buttercream is well mixed.

3. Refrigerate buttercream in a covered container until ready to use. This will keep at least 2 weeks. Before using, allow to soften to room temperature and beat for a moment, if necessary, to make more spreadable.

1¾ cups buttercream

Italian Meringue

1⅓ cups sugar
⅔ cup water
¼ teaspoon cream of tartar
4 egg whites
⅛ teaspoon salt
⅛ teaspoon lemon extract

1. In a small, heavy saucepan, combine sugar, water, and cream of tartar, stirring over low heat until sugar is dissolved.

2. Cover saucepan and bring mixture to boiling. Boil gently 5 minutes. Uncover and put candy thermometer in place. During cooking, wash sugar crystals from sides of pan with a pastry brush dipped in water. Cook without stirring until mixture reaches 240°F.

3. While syrup is cooking, beat egg whites, using electric mixer, until peaks are stiff, but not dry. Beating constantly, pour hot syrup over beaten egg whites in a thin, steady stream (do not scrape pan).

4. After all the hot syrup is added, add salt and lemon extract. Continue beating 4 minutes, or until meringue stiffens. Use immediately.

Fruit-Glazed Layer Cake

Cake:
1 cup plus 2 tablespoons sifted cake flour
⅛ teaspoon salt
4 egg yolks
⅓ cup cool water
1 cup sugar
1 teaspoon orange extract
½ teaspoon lemon extract
4 egg whites
½ teaspoon cream of tartar
Vanilla Buttercream

Fruit Glaze:
1 tablespoon sugar
2 teaspoons cornstarch
⅓ cup apricot syrup
3 tablespoons pineapple syrup
1 tablespoon lemon juice
1 cup coarsely chopped walnuts
10 to 12 medium-size strawberries
1 slice canned pineapple
5 or 6 canned apricot halves (optional)
14 to 18 seedless grapes

1. For cake, blend flour with salt; set aside. Beat egg yolks until very thick and lemon colored. Add cool water a little at a time, beating well after each addition. Add sugar gradually, beating after each addition. Beat in extracts.

2. Sift the dry ingredients over egg mixture about one fourth at a time; after each addition gently fold in until blended.

3. Using a clean bowl and beaters, beat egg whites until frothy. Beat in cream of tartar. Continue beating until stiff, not dry, peaks form. Carefully fold beaten egg whites into the egg yolk mixture until just blended.

4. Turn batter into 2 ungreased 8-inch round layer cake pans and spread batter evenly.

5. Bake at 325°F about 25 minutes, or until cake tests done. Invert over wire racks (cake should not touch rack); cool layers about 1 hour before removing from pans.

6. Slice each layer in half horizontally, forming 4 layers. Place 1 layer on a serving plate. Spread top with ⅓ cup vanilla buttercream. Put second and third layers in place, frosting the tops of each

layer. Place fourth layer on top and leave unfrosted. Use remaining buttercream to frost side of cake, smoothing as much as possible. Chill about 15 minutes.

7. For glaze, combine sugar and cornstarch in a small saucepan. Add apricot syrup, pineapple syrup, and lemon juice. Cook over medium-high heat, stirring constantly, until mixture thickens and begins to boil. Boil 1 minute; cool.

8. Gently press walnuts into buttercream on side of cake, a handful at a time. Place pineapple slice in center of top layer. Place a whole strawberry in center of the pineapple slice, and place grapes in a circle around the pineapple. If desired, cut apricot halves in half and place apricots end-to-end in a circle around the grapes. Place strawberry halves around edge of top layer.

9. Brush glaze over fruit, trying to keep glaze from drizzling down side of cake.

10. Using a pastry bag and tube 14 or 15 (star), fill with remaining buttercream. Pipe a shell border around top and bottom edges of cake. Chill briefly.

One 8-inch layer cake

Note: Any combination of fruit may be used, but syrup from canned apricots and pineapple is needed for the glaze.

Vanilla Buttercream

4 egg yolks
½ cup sugar
½ cup hot half-and-half
2 teaspoons vanilla extract
1 cup chilled unsalted butter

1. Put egg yolks and sugar into a bowl and beat until thick. Add hot half-and-half gradually, beating constantly. Pour into a saucepan. Cook and stir about 5 minutes, or until thickened.

2. Remove from heat and stir in vanilla extract. Pour into a bowl and beat 1 minute to cool slightly. Add butter, a small amount at a time, beating until butter is melted after each addition. Cool.

About 2 cups buttercream

Complicated Outside
Decorated Cakes

In this chapter and the two following, food coloring is added to cake icing and decorations with excellent effect. Food coloring is easy and fun to use, and can add greatly to the beauty and reality of your icings and decorations if used judiciously.

There are three primary colors: red, blue, and yellow; when mixed they produce the secondary colors as follows:

red plus blue = violet
red plus yellow = orange
yellow plus blue = green

We suggest that you purchase a minimum of four colors: the three primary colors plus green, since the latter is used so often in decorations. To vary your green color, a small amount of red or chocolate added to the icing along with the green will darken it slightly.

Food coloring is available in paste and liquid forms, but most decorators prefer paste, since the thicker paste texture doesn't thin icing down as much as the liquid tends to do.

If paste colors dry up on your shelf, simply stir in a few drops of medicinal glycerine (ask your druggist) to reconstitute the texture.

All food colors, whether paste or liquid, deepen slightly on standing, once they've been mixed with icing. Remember to add colors with caution. Food coloring is like salt; you can put it in easily enough, but you can't take it out.

Add coloring bit by bit, mixing well after each drop. As soon as the desired shade is reached, stop adding coloring. At this point, some decorators like to leave their icing overnight in the refrigerator to see how the shades have darkened by the next day.

If the icings have turned too dark, do not add new, uncolored icing to them in an attempt to lighten them. Instead, spoon a small amount of the darkened icing into some new, uncolored icing and stir; continue adding colored icing, spoonful by spoonful, until the desired shade is reached.

If liquid food colors thin down the icing to an undesirable piping texture, beat in some confectioners' sugar, little by little, until the desired texture is reached.

CAKES DECORATED WITH MARZIPAN

Marzipan is candy, and nothing is more fun than making something both beautiful and edible at the same time. Marzipan fruits, vegetables, and flowers look difficult to make, but are actually very easy. You don't have to have any manual talent, so if you were terrible at modeling clay as a child, you will still be able to do beautiful work with only a little patience. Most novices, in fact, are amazed at their first-time results.

With results practically guaranteed, then, all you'll need are a few rules to insure professional results, even the first time:

1. Roses and other flowers made of marzipan look lovely with marzipan stems and leaves. Fruits and vegetables look their best if their leaves and stems are bought commercially.

2. Use paste colors rather than liquid colors when possible. Paste colors are very concentrated, and only a little is needed to give the desired color; besides this, paste colors are available in a large number of colors; much less mixing of colors is needed than with liquid colors.

3. Work from nature when possible. Have a strawberry or a carrot or lemon in front of you as you model.

4. Don't be restricted by these instructions. Anything that can be modeled of marzipan, from turnips to mangoes, will, if recognizable, enhance your finished cake. Just remember to use your decoration with integrity; for example, put your carrots on a carrot cake.

Carrot Cake with Candy Carrots

Cake:

    3 eggs plus 1 yolk
    2 cups lightly packed brown sugar
 1½ cups cooking oil
    2 cups sifted all-purpose flour
    2 teaspoons baking powder
 1½ teaspoons baking soda
    ¾ teaspoon salt
    2 teaspoons cinnamon
  1/8 teaspoon allspice

1. For cake, beat eggs and yolk in large bowl of an electric mixer. Add brown sugar and beat well. Add oil and continue beating until well mixed.

2. Meanwhile, sift flour with baking powder, baking soda, salt, cinnamon, and allspice. Add to batter, mixing well.

3. Add carrots, walnuts, and pineapple to batter; mix well and spoon into a well-greased 10-inch springform pan which has been lined on the bottom with greased parchment paper.

2 cups grated pared carrots
1 cup chopped walnuts
1 can (8 ounces) unsweetened
    crushed pineapple (undrained)

Frosting:
¾ cup butter
4½ ounces cream cheese
¾ teaspoon vanilla extract
1½ pounds confectioners' sugar
    (about 5 to 6 cups)
1/8 teaspoon salt
1 can (8 ounces) unsweetened
    crushed pineapple (undrained)
24 Marzipan Candy Carrots

4. Bake at 350°F 60 to 65 minutes, or until cake tests done. Turn cake out on a wire rack to cool.
5. For frosting, cream butter and cream cheese until well mixed in small bowl of an electric mixer. Add vanilla extract and mix well, then add confectioners' sugar and salt, mixing well again.
6. Drain pineapple, pressing pulp to extract the juice until the pulp is very dry. Measure 1/3 cup pineapple juice and blend with 1 cup of the frosting. Put 1 cup of the frosting into a small bowl and mix in the drained pineapple.
7. Split the cake in half horizontally with a long-bladed, serrated knife. Set bottom layer on a serving plate. Cover with the frosting containing the pineapple. Top cake with second layer. Then cover top and sides of cake with frosting, making it as smooth as possible. Dip knife blade in hot water from time to time, if desired, to insure smoothness. Refrigerate until frosting hardens.
8. Arrange the 12 pairs of Marzipan Candy Carrots in spoke fashion around cake, stem side out.

One 10-inch cake

Marzipan Candy Carrots

¼ cup canned almond paste
2 teaspoons light corn syrup
3 tablespoons (scant)
    marshmallow creme
2/3 cup confectioners' sugar (more
    if needed)
    Yellow food coloring
    Red food coloring
1 teaspoon unsweetened cocoa
24 marzipan carrot stems

1. Mix almond paste, corn syrup, marshmallow creme, and confectioners' sugar together with fingers in a bowl, until well combined and smooth; knead in a little extra confectioners' sugar if paste is sticky. There will be about 10 tablespoons marzipan paste.
2. Form paste into a ball and knead in a very small amount of yellow coloring, then knead in a little red coloring to make an orange-colored paste. Knead well, adding a little confectioners' sugar if paste is sticky. When a recognizable orange color results, reform paste into a ball.
3. Divide ball into quarters, then cut each quarter into 3 pieces. Model each piece into a pair of carrots, making uneven sizes; one carrot should be chunky and thick, the other, long, thin, and pointed at the end.
4. Use a wooden pick to make flat lines across top of carrot (see illustration). Add stems, shiny side up. Arrange in pairs on a tray and cover tray. Refrigerate until ready to use.
Note: If you wish to make your own leaves, make up a small batch of marzipan (page 50) and color it a pale shade of green. See Marzipan Decorations (page 49) for instructions on making leaves.

This frosted chocolate layer cake, lusciouis enough by itself, is made extra special when enclosed in chocolate. It appears to be complicated, but is not at all difficult to make. A sprinkling of confectioners' sugar is the finishing touch to this chocolate lover's delight.

Chocolate Cake with Molded Topping

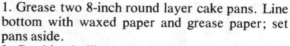

¾ cup boiling water
3 ounces (3 squares) unsweetened chocolate
2¼ cups sifted cake flour
1 teaspoon baking soda
1½ teaspoons baking powder
1 teaspoon salt
⅔ cup butter or margarine
1½ cups firmly packed brown sugar
2 teaspoons vanilla extract
3 eggs, well beaten
¾ cup buttermilk
   Cocoa-Chocolate Buttercream
   Molded Topping
1 tablespoon confectioners' sugar

1. Grease two 8-inch round layer cake pans. Line bottom with waxed paper and grease paper; set pans aside.
2. Combine boiling water and chocolate, stir until thick, and set aside.
3. Sift together flour, baking soda, baking powder, and salt; set aside.
4. Cream together butter, brown sugar, and vanilla extract until creamy and smooth. Add eggs, beating until fluffy. Add melted chocolate; stir to blend. Add sifted dry ingredients in thirds alternately with buttermilk, beating gently after each addition. Turn batter into prepared pans.
5. Bake at 350°F 35 to 40 minutes, or until cake tests done. Cool 10 minutes. Turn layers out onto wire racks, remove paper, and cool completely.
6. Place 1 cake layer on a serving plate. Spread generously with buttercream and top with other layer. Frost entire cake with buttercream and refrigerate until ready to cover with chocolate sheets.
7. Make molded topping, roll out as directed and refrigerate, for about 10 minutes. Then remove 1 sheet of chocolate from refrigerator and peel off top layer of paper. Check for pliability. Chocolate sheet may need to be returned to refrigerator for a moment; or it may be too stiff. If this is the case, allow to soften at room temperature for a moment, then test. Chocolate should be pliable enough to begin bending if lifted. Use spatula to loosen chocolate from bottom layer of paper.
8. Lift paper and chocolate together and place on side of cake, using hands to gently ease and mold chocolate to side. Chocolate will fall by itself, stiffly onto top of cake as picture, but you can help it (gently) as needed. Repeat with remaining 2 sheets of chocolate until cake is completely covered. Refrigerate cake immediately, for 20 minutes. At serving time, sift a little confectioner's sugar over top for decoration.

One 8-inch layer cake

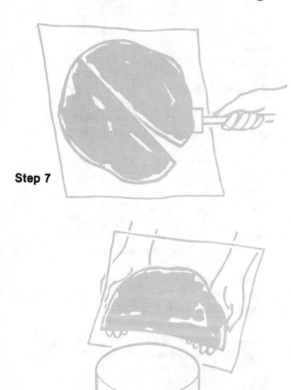

Step 7

Step 8

Cocoa-Chocolate Buttercream

¾ cup butter
¾ cup firmly packed dark brown sugar
1 egg yolk
1 tablespoon rum
　Pinch salt
2 tablespoons unsweetened cocoa
½ cup semisweet chocolate pieces

1. Beat butter in large bowl of electric mixer until fluffy. Add brown sugar, beating well. Add egg yolk, rum, salt, and cocoa, mixing well.
2. Melt chocolate pieces over simmering water. Cool slightly and add to butter-brown sugar mixture, beating thoroughly.
3. Buttercream will keep several days in a covered container in refrigerator. Beat just until smooth before using.

2 cups

Molded Topping

1 cup sliced blanched almonds
　Cooking oil
1 cup sugar
1¼ cups semisweet chocolate pieces

1. Place almonds in a single layer in 15×10×1-inch jelly-roll pan. Set in a 350°F oven about 10 minutes, or until almonds are lightly toasted. Remove from pan.
2. Line same pan with a layer of aluminum foil and brush bottom of foil with oil, coating well. Lay toasted almonds in center of pan.
3. Heat sugar in a heavy saucepan over low heat, stirring constantly with a wooden spoon, until completely liquefied and golden brown. Immediately pour sugar syrup over almonds and allow to harden.
4. Break almond brittle into small pieces. Put pieces through coarsest blade of food chopper or chop, a little at a time, in blender to a coarse powder.
5. Melt chocolate pieces in top of double boiler over simmering water. When just melted, add almond brittle powder and mix well.
6. Pour ½ cup of chocolate mixture onto a 12-inch square of waxed paper. Cover chocolate mixture with another square of waxed paper. Using a rolling pin, roll out to a very thin circle, about 11 inches in diameter. (Coarse bits in chocolate may make little holes in waxed paper, but continue rolling.)
7. Leave rolled-out chocolate mixture in waxed paper and place on cookie sheet. Repeat rolling out procedure 2 more times, with remaining chocolate mixture. Stack waxed-paper-covered chocolate sheets on top of each other and refrigerate 10 minutes.

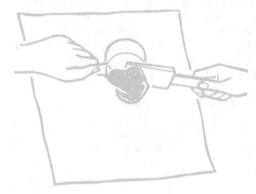

Step 6

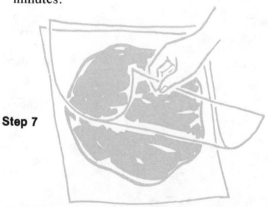

Step 7

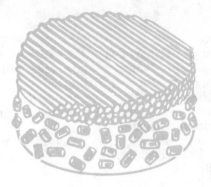

A cake decorated with chocolate curls is lovely to see and the curls are not difficult to make, but they're a little time consuming. Sometimes it takes a long time for the chocolate to dry and cool sufficiently for the curls to be made.

Choose a dry, stay-at-home-day for your first attempt, and double the recipe for practice, if desired. One of the many nice things about chocolate curls is that they can be made ahead and stored for days, if covered and kept in a cool, dry place. Any broken pieces or scrapings can be used to decorate the sides of a cake.

Chocolate Cake with Chocolate Curls

Chocolate Cake (page 32)
Chocolate Buttercream (page 24)
Chocolate Curls
1 ounce dark sweet chocolate
Confectioners' sugar for sprinkling top

1. Lay 1 cake layer on a serving plate and cover with buttercream. Top with second layer; then cover top and sides of whole cake with remaining buttercream.
2. Arrange a parallel row of chocolate curls across top of cake. If any extra curls remain, heap them up in center; but be sure that all curls run in the same direction and are parallel to each other.
3. Press any remaining bits of curls or scrapings of chocolate against sides of cake, grating an additional ounce of dark sweet chocolate, if needed, to cover sides completely.
4. Sift confectioners' sugar lightly over top of cake. If desired, lay 2 paper strips almost at right angles to curls. Sift confectioners' sugar over top, then remove strips for striped pattern.

One 8-inch layer cake

Chocolate Curls

4 ounces (1 bar) dark sweet chocolate, grated

1. Place grated chocolate in top of double boiler over hot water until just melted. Stir well with wooden spoon.
2. Spoon one quarter of chocolate directly onto formica-topped table (or any flat-topped table; candy makers use a marble slab), then spoon remaining three quarters of chocolate onto 3 separate areas on table.
3. With a rubber spatula, spread chocolate mounds out in all directions to form 4 rough squares of chocolate. Keep pushing and working chocolate out further with spatula until squares are as big as possible and chocolate will not spread any further.
4. Allow chocolate to cool. This may take anywhere from 20 minutes to several hours, depending on heat and humidity.
5. After chocolate has begun to cool and dry, check it from time to time. User a decorator's spatula (see illustration), to see if chocolate is ready; if chocolate is too soft, it will stick to spatula.
6. To make curls, half scrape, half push decora-

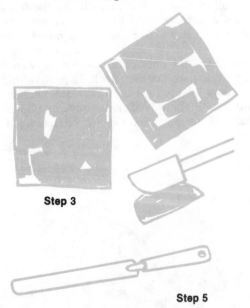

Step 3

Step 5

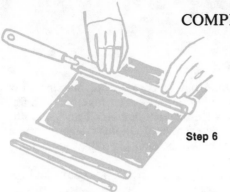

Step 6

tor's spatula along top of chocolate as in illustration. With a little pressure, curls will just about form themselves.

7. Set formed curls on a tray or plate lined with waxed paper. Use to decorate top of cake. Reserve any scrapings or broken pieces of curls to press against sides of cake. Curls will keep for some time in a cool, dry place.

Chocolate Potato Cake with Marzipan

Chocolate Potato Cake
Marzipan Filling and Potatoes
Chocolate Fudge Frosting
(page 20)

1. Prepare Chocolate Potato Cake and marzipan.
2. Place ½ cup marzipan between two sheets of waxed paper that have been sprinkled liberally with **confectioners' sugar;** roll out marzipan to an 8-inch square, cutting and piecing, if necessary to form a square.
3. Place 1 layer of cake on a serving plate. Peel top sheet of waxed paper off of marzipan square. Invert marzipan (still attached to one sheet of waxed paper) onto cake layer; then remove second sheet of waxed paper.
4. Use a spatula to cover layer of marzipan with fudge frosting. Then set second layer in place. Cover top and sides of cake with remaining frosting. Let frosting set.
5. At serving time, pile marzipan potatoes in center of cake.

One 8-inch square layer cake

Chocolate Potato Cake

¾	**cup butter**
1	**cup sugar**
4	**egg yolks**
3	**ounces (3 squares) unsweetened chocolate, melted**
1	**tablespoon vanilla extract**
1½	**cups unseasoned mashed potatoes (see Note)**
5	**egg whites**
⅔	**cup sugar**
1	**cup ground almonds**
3	**cups sifted cake flour**
1	**teaspoon baking powder**
¼	**teaspoon salt**

1. Beat butter in large bowl of electric mixer, then add 1 cup sugar and cream well. Add egg yolks, one at a time, beating well after each addition. Then, with beaters still running, add melted chocolate, vanilla extract, and mashed pototoes; mix well.
2. Beat egg whites until they hold soft peaks; then add ⅔ cup sugar, a little at a time, beating well after each addition, until mixture is stiff. Fold this meringue into chocolate batter, mixing until almost blended. Then fold in almonds the same way.
3. Put flour, baking powder, and salt into a sifter; sift it over top of batter, a little at a time, folding after each addition.
4. Divide batter evenly between two 8-inch square baking pans that have been well greased and then lined on the bottom with greased parchment paper.
5. Bake at 350°F about 30 minutes, or until cake tests done. Turn out on wire racks to cool.

Note: If you use instant mashed potaotes, make them of medium consistency, using only water; omit salt, butter, and milk.

Marzipan Filling and Potatoes

6 tablespoons canned almond paste
1 tablespoon light corn syrup
¼ cup marshmallow creme
1 cup confectioners' sugar (more if needed)
Unsweetened cocoa (about 2 tablespoons)

1. Mix almond paste, corn syrup, marshmallow creme, and confectioners' sugar together with fingers in a bowl until well combined and smooth; knead in a little extra confectioners' sugar if paste is sticky. There will be about 15 tablespoons marzipan paste.

2. Measure out ½ cup (packed measure) and reserve for filling.

3. For marzipan potatoes, divide remaining marzipan into small pieces, about ½ teaspoon each. Form each piece into a rough oval, to resemble the shape of an Idaho potato. Have a potato to look at as you work.

4. Use pointed end of a wooden skewer to press several "eyes" into each potato. Roll potatoes in cocoa, then brush off excess cocoa. Set potatoes in a single layer on a waxed paper-covered plate; slip into a plastic bag and close with a twist tie until ready to use.

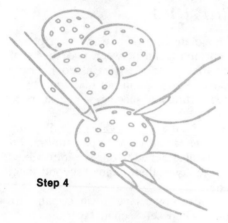

Step 4

Easter Hat with Marzipan Roses

White Sheet Cake (page 34; use vanilla extract instead of lemon extract)
Vanilla Buttercream (page 40; 1½ recipes)
Pink marzipan hatband
10 pink marzipan roses
12 marzipan leaves
Green marzipan for stems
Spun Sugar Threads, optional

1. Cut 3 rounds from cake, using a 9-inch layer cake pan as pattern for one and make 2 small rounds, using a 5-inch plate for pattern.

2. Set the 9-inch layer on a serving plate and cover top with Vanilla Buttercream. Place 1 small layer in center of large layer and cover top with buttercream. Place remaining layer on top and cover entire cake with remaining buttercream; smooth icing on top and sides with a metal spatula dipped in hot water.

3. Prepare Marzipan Decorations. Press a 22-inch marzipan strip around bottom 5-inch layer, crossing over at ends, forming the hatband. Refrigerate cake at least 1 hour.

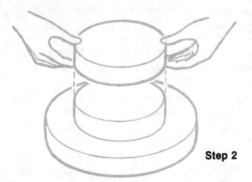

Step 2

Step 3

4. When cake is thoroughly chilled, arrange roses and leaves around hatband. Use green marzipan ropes to form stems, curling them out from under

Basket Cake 68
Snow Queen Doll Cake 62
Train Cake 31

Step 4

roses (see illustration). If any green marzipan remains, shape tiny leaves and buds and attach to stems.

5. If desired, cover roses and leaves with Spun Sugar Threads.

One 3-layer hat cake

Marzipan Decorations

6 tablespoons canned almond paste
1 tablespoon light corn syrup
¼ cup marshmallow creme
1 cup confectioners' sugar (more if needed)
Red food coloring
Green food coloring
Glaze for marzipan (page 54), optional

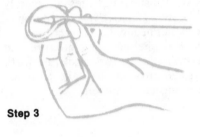

Step 3

1. Mix almond paste, corn syrup, and marshmallow creme. Add confectioners' sugar, ½ cup at a time, kneading until smooth and adding additional confectioners' sugar until no longer sticky, if necessary.

2. Measure ¼ cup marzipan by packing it into a measuring cup. Blend in red food coloring to color pink for hatband. Set aside.

3. To make roses, measure ½ cup marzipan and tint very pale pink by blending in less red food coloring than used for ¼ cup marzipan. Cut and roll into 10 equal-sized balls. Slice each ball into 9 pieces about the same size. Flatten each piece on the counter or other flat surface with your hand, to form irregularly shaped circles, ¾ to 1¼ inches in diameter. (If pieces stick to surface, sprinkle surface with confectioners sugar.) Remove with a metal spatula. Wind one of the smaller circles around the pointed end of a wooden skewer or orange stick coated with confectioners' sugar. Wind remaining "petals" on the skewer, overlapping them, using the smaller ones first (see illustration). Squeeze tightly so petals adhere to each other. Pinch bottom of flower slightly and remove skewer. Set aside on waxed paper and form remaining nine roses in same manner.

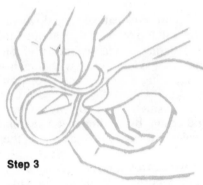

Step 3

Step 3

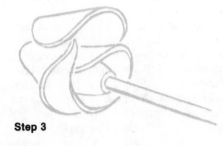

Step 3

4. Tint remaining marzipan green to make leaves and stems. Measure 2 tablespoons marzipan for leaves and place remaining marzipan in a plastic

Step 4

bag and refrigerate. Roll green marzipan paste into about a dozen equal-sized balls. Flatten each ball to form leaves, about 1½×1 inches. Using fork tines or a wooden pick, press indentations into surface of each leaf (see illustration).

5. If desired, roses and leaves may be glazed (page 54). Paint hot glaze with artists' brush over entire surface or roses and leaves, and place on waxed paper to dry overnight. If not glazed, roses and leaves may be placed on cake without drying.

6. Put a strip of darker pink marzipan between 2 long pieces of waxed paper sprinkled with confectioners' sugar and roll into a strip 22 inches long and 1¼ inches wide. Cut a "V" out of both ends as for a gift ribbon.

7. Form remaining green marzipan into long thin ropes for stems and, if desired, tendrils.

Spun Sugar Threads

1 cup granulated sugar
1 tablespoon light corn syrup

1. Cover working surface with newspaper. Set decorated cake on it.

2. Mix sugar with corn syrup in a heavy skillet; place over low heat. Stir mixture constantly with a wooden spoon just until sugar liquefies completely and turns golden brown. Remove from heat immediately and place skillet near cake.

3. Dip a table fork in melted sugar mixture and drain off excess drops. Move fork back and forth rapidly over roses all around the cake to make sugar threads, forming a delicate veil.

Cornucopia Cake

Buttermilk Layer Cake
Buttercream Decorating Frosting
Cornucopia
Assorted Marzipan Fruits

1. Place 1 layer of buttermilk cake upside down on a serving plate. Spread top of layer with about 1 to 1½ cups yellow frosting. Place second layer on top, right side up. Frost sides of cake with remaining yellow frosting, using a metal spatula to form swirls.

2. Frost top of cake, using about 1 cup white frosting. Form a spiral design by holding metal spatula flat in center of cake and moving it outward as the cake is rotated.

3. Pipe stiffened white frosting through a pastry bag with tube 22 in a border around bottom edge of cake. Pipe a border around top of cake using tube 19.

4. Arrange the Cornucopia. Put a spoonful of buttercream frosting, or icing remaining from cornucopia, onto cake and set cornucopia in place, with pointed end turned up. Fill opening with marzipan fruits, and place some spilling out onto cake top. Pipe green frosting through tube 67 forming leaves directly on marzipan wherever desired.

One 10-inch layer cake

Buttermilk Layer Cake

4½ cups sifted cake flour
1 tablespoon baking powder
1 teaspoon baking soda
½ teaspoon salt
¾ cup butter
2½ teaspoons vanilla extract
2¼ cups sugar
3 eggs
2¼ cups buttermilk

1. Sift flour with baking powder, baking soda, and salt; set aside.
2. Cream butter with vanilla extract until softened. Add sugar gradually, creaming until fluffy after each addition. Add eggs, one at a time, beating thoroughly after each is added.
3. Alternately add dry ingredients in fourths and buttermilk in thirds, beating only until smooth after each addition. Pour batter into 2 greased and floured 10-inch round layer cake pans.
4. Bake at 350°F 35 to 40 minutes, or until cake tests done.
5. Cool cake in pans on wire rack 10 minutes. Loosen edges with a spatula, remove cake from pans, and cool completely on wire racks.

Buttercream Decorating Frosting

1½ cups vegetable shortening
¾ cup butter or margarine
1 tablespoon lemon extract
9 cups sifted confectioners' sugar (about)
Yellow food coloring
Green food coloring

1. In large bowl of an electric mixer, beat together shortening, butter, and lemon extract.
2. Gradually beat in confectioners' sugar until frosting is of spreading consistency. Tint 4 cups frosting with yellow food coloring for filling cake and frosting sides.
3. Remaining frosting should hold its shape when piped through a pastry tube. If necessary, beat in additional confectioners' sugar to stiffen. Tint 2 tablespoons frosting with green food coloring to make leaves, and leave remaining frosting white.

About 7 cups frosting

Cornucopia

Aluminum foil
Royal Icing:
2 large egg whites
3½ cups sifted confectioners' sugar (more if needed)
1 teaspoon lemon juice or ⅛ teaspoon cream of tartar
Yellow food coloring

1. Cut three 12×9-inch pieces of aluminum foil. Cut again diagonally to form 6 triangles. Lay foil pieces together to form one triangle, 6 layers thick.
2. Form into cone shape, wide at one end, closed at the other. Bend tip of cornucopia up slightly, and stuff with crumbled aluminum foil for added strength. Trim wide end of cone with a scissors to make a neat, even-looking opening.
3. Beat egg whites slightly in small bowl of an electric mixer. Add 2 tablespoons confectioners' sugar and beat at high speed about 2 minutes.
4. Gradually add more confectioners' sugar, beating until mixture will hold its shape. Beat in lemon juice and tint with food coloring. Beat again if icing becomes lumpy.
5. Place cornucopia mold on neck of a carbonated beverage bottle. Using a pastry bag and tube 17, cover cornucopia with icing, starting at wide part of cone and forming continuous rings around circumference of cone. Allow to dry. If desired, when outside is dry, spread any remaining icing inside cone to cover aluminum foil.

Note: If necessary, keep icing covered with a damp cloth until used.

Assorted Marzipan Fruits

¾ cup canned almond paste, cut in
    small pieces
2 tablespoons light corn syrup
½ cup marshmallow creme
2 cups confectioners' sugar (more
    if needed)
   Paste food coloring
   Liquid red food coloring
   Confectioners' sugar
   Assorted artificial fruit leaves
   Glaze for Marzipan
   Red decorator sugar
   Whole cloves, rounded top part
    removed
1 ounce dark sweet chocolate,
    melted

1. Mix almond paste, corn syrup, and marshmallow creme until well combined. Add confectioners' sugar, ½ cup at a time, kneading until smooth after each addition, until marzipan is no longer sticky.
2. Divide into as many portions as colors desired. Blend paste food coloring into each portion, and shape into selected fruits. Let shaped pieces dry uncovered at room temperature at least 6 hours.
3. Compete assembly of fruits with glaze, fruit leaves, and other finishes.

About 25 to 30 pieces marzipan

UNTINTED MARZIPAN

Peaches: Roll about 2 teaspoons marzipan into a ball. Elongate slightly to form peach shape. Using a flat wooden stick or back of a knife blade, make characteristic side indentations. Mix a few drops of red food coloring with a few teaspoons of water. Using a tiny paintbrush, brush on "blush" on one side of peach. When "blush" dries, roll peach in confectioners' sugar, removing excess with a cotton swab. Add a stem and leaf to each peach, but do not glaze.

Strawberries: Roll about 1 teaspoon marzipan into a ball. Pinch bottom, shaping ball into a strawberry shape. Dip entire strawberry in glaze and roll in red sugar until completely covered. Insert strawberry leaves and set aside to dry.

GREEN MARZIPAN

Limes: Roll about 1½ teaspoons marzipan into a ball. Use a frog or a fine grater to give citrus-fruit texture. Make a crossed indentation at one end and insert a clove. Paint entire surface with glaze and set aside to dry.

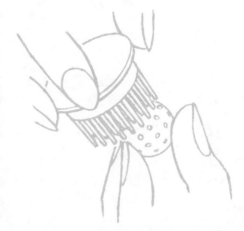

Grape leaves: Roll about 1 teaspoon marzipan into a ball. Flatten into a leaf shape about 1¾×1 inch. Press crossed end of clove into each leaf, forming a stem. Use as base for grapes.

PURPLE MARZIPAN

Grapes: Using about 1 teaspoon marzipan, pinch off small pieces to form grapes about the size of small dried peas. Paint grape leaf (see Green Marzipan) with glaze and place a single layer of grapes on leaf, as close to each other as possible. Glaze grapes and place another layer on top of first. Continue this procedure until a high cluster of grapes is formed. Glaze top surface and set aside to dry.

Plums: Roll about 1½ teaspoons marzipan into a ball. Using a flat wooden stick or back of a knife blade, make characteristic indentations on sides. Slightly press top to flatten a little. Roll in confectioners' sugar, removing excess with a cotton swab. Press leaf in top, paint a spot of glaze only on front, and set aside to dry.

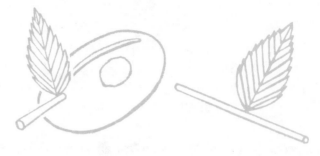

Cherries: Roll about 1 teaspoon marzipan into a ball. Make a slight indentation on top. Paint entire surface with undiluted liquid red food coloring and set on waxed paper to dry. Paint entire surface with glaze, insert cherry leaf, and set aside to dry.

YELLOW MARZIPAN

Bananas: Shape about 2 teaspoons marzipan to form a banana. Paint ends and streaks on sides, using a tiny paintbrush and melted chocolate. Insert crossed end of clove in one end of banana, paint entire surface with glaze, and set aside to dry.

Lemons: Roll about 1½ teaspoons marzipan into a ball. Use a frog or a fine grater to give citrus-fruit texture. Make a crossed indentation at one end and insert a clove. Paint entire surface with glaze and set aside to dry.

Pears: Roll about 2 teaspoons marzipan into a ball, pinching to make top thinner than bottom. Press clove into bottom of pear. Mix a few drops red food coloring with a few teaspoons water and paint a "blush" on one side of pear, using a tiny paintbrush. Fasten pear leaves, paint entire surface with glaze, and set aside to dry.

ORANGE MARZIPAN

Oranges: Roll about 2 teaspoons marzipan into a ball. Use a frog or a fine grater to give citrus-fruit texture. Make a crossed indentation at one end, and insert a clove. Paint entire surface with glaze and set aside to dry.

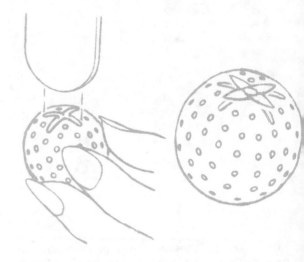

Pumpkins: Roll about 1½ tablespoons marzipan into a ball. Press top in slightly and make characteristic ridges in pumpkin, using a flat wooden stick or back of a knife blade. Press crossed end of clove into top, forming stem. Paint entire surface with glaze, and set aside to dry.

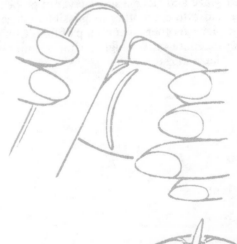

Glaze for Marzipan

- **3 tablespoons light corn syrup**
- **3 tablespoons sugar**
- **4 tablespoons water**

Combine ingredients in small saucepan; heat to boiling. With artist's brush, paint hot glaze over fruit. Set aside to dry.

Simple and Complicated
Pastry Tube Decorations

Pastry tubes are actually tiny funnels which yield special designs when icing is forced through them; the shape of the metal tube determines the kind and size of the design. There are dozens of different pastry tubes, each with a definite purpose; these purposes range from making the simplest dots to the most complicated flower petals. Each tube, in fact, can be used to make many different designs, depending on the pressure and directions applied to the tube. But in the following chapter we have limited those few tubes used to their basic designs.

Using the simpler pastry tubes is not hard to learn. Even if you've never used a tube before, after a few moments' practice on a sheet of waxed paper, you should have no trouble decorating a cake. To reassure you further, the following cakes were planned with the beginner in mind; beforehand practice is actually written into the instructions.

A word of advice: Practice very slowly and allow yourself to make mistakes. Everyone does, even the professionals. Patience with yourself is an important as practice.

●

Assemble and check the ingredients and equipment.

1. Buttercream (or other icing) must be soft enough to move easily through the tube, but not so soft that designs don't keep their shape. If the icing has been refrigerated for any length of time, beat it with an electric mixer (or by hand) until of piping consistency. (Check this by pushing it through a tube.) If the icing is too soft, refrigerate it until hard enough to use.

2. Lay out a sheet of waxed paper on a flat surface, or use a tray or inverted cookie sheet for a practice piping surface.

3. Check the recipe for required tubes and be sure each one is clean.

4. Assemble parchment pastry bags (instructions on page 59).

Practice using tubes.

1. Pack a tube full of buttercream and hold the filled tube between the thumb and middle fingertip; use index finger to push out desired design. Practice until you can make the designs to your satisfaction.

2. After mastering finger pressure, drop tube in pastry bag and fill with icing. Hold top of pastry bag with one hand and apply pressure, while the other hand acts as a guide. Practice applying pressure to the pastry bag, until the pipings are successful. When the waxed paper sheet is full of pipings, scrape them off and return icing to bowl.

3. If tubes clog at any time, carefully use a wooden pick to clear tubes. Don't poke sharp objects into tubes, as this can bend the openings out of shape.

4. Clean tubes with hot water, detergent, and a small artist's brush. (Or buy a tiny brush available for this purpose.) Rinse tubes carefully and allow them to dry in an upright position on paper toweling.

Individual tubes

1. **Plain tubes** have round holes, ranging from very tiny to very large. For our purpose, they can make straight and wavy stem lines, block letters, S lines, dots, and dot bouquets.

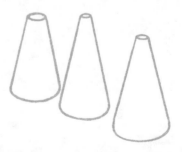

To make straight and wavy stem lines, block letters, and S lines: Hold bag with tip of tube just barely touching surface and tilted slightly as illustrated. Exert a steady, even pressure with index finger, moving slowly to form the line. Use your

entire arm to make lines, bending it only at the elbow. Start vertical lines at top, piping downward; stop pressure and lift tube off at bottom of line. Practice making straight and curved lines on waxed paper, in every direction. Practice making block letters by piping the alphabet slowly onto

waxed paper, remembering to start all vertical lines at the top. Practice S lines by making a row of S's as illustrated. When satisfied, pipe lines and letters onto cake.

To pipe dots: Point tube at a 90° angle to the waxed paper, as illustrated. Tip of tube should be

just barely touching surface. With index finger pressure, squeeze out a dot of icing, lifting tube slightly but not removing it from dot. Lift tube away from dot after you stop pressure. Practice making a series of individual dots. Then make a

row of dots, touching, but not crowding each other. When satisfied, pipe dots onto cake.

To make dot bouquets: Pipe a small circle of dots, then fill it in with more dots. Use a tiny plain tube to pipe a row of stems together. If desired, fill a small, plain tube with icing in a contrasting color and pipe tiny centers to the flowers.

2. **Star tubes** have an even bigger range than plain tubes, and an enormous number of purposes. To the novice, these are the most useful for piping simple stars and rosettes, although they can also make very effective straight, wavy, and S lines with a serrated texture.

To make stars: Point filled bag straight up and down as for dots, at a 90° angle to waxed-paper surface. Tube should be just barely touching surface. Exert slight pressure for an instant to squeeze out a star, meanwhile lifting the tube slightly but not removing from star. Lift tube away from star after you stop pressure. Practice making a row of stars on waxed paper. Then add to cake as desired.

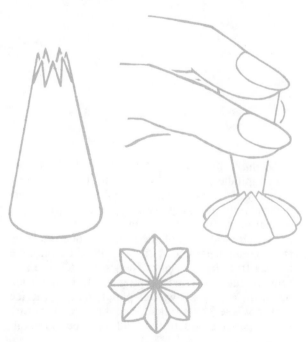

To make rosettes: Hold bag exactly as for stars and exert pressure for an instant. Instead of raising tube slightly as in stars, give it a slight turn to the right; then stop pressure and remove tube. Practice making a row of rosettes on waxed paper. When satisfied, pipe rosettes onto cake.

Note: A number of other tubes are available for making simple drop flowers (made the same way as stars and rosettes) and these can easily substitute anywhere in this chapter for rosettes. If desired, buy tubes 96, 129, 171, 177, 135 through 140, 190, and 193. Drop flowers, like rosettes, can be even more effective if you add a tiny center dot in a contrasting color.

3. **Flower tubes** come in a large range of sizes and shapes, some curved, some straight, some in a double curve for making elaborately shaped petals. For our purposes, we use only one curved flower tube for shamrock petals, and one straight flower tube for rose petals.

To make shamrock petals: Hold filled bag between middle joints of fingers. Hold tube as illustrated, wide end down and touching waxed paper, narrow end raised slightly and pointing left. Begin pressure, swinging tube slightly to right as you press. The wide end of the tube, the one touching the waxed paper, will act as a pivot while the tube swings from left to right. Then stop pressure and remove tube. Practice piping several shamrock petals in a row on waxed paper. Then practice piping whole shamrocks. Pipe first petal, rotate waxed paper as illustrated, and pipe second petal.

Repeat with rotation and piping until all three petals have been piped (or pipe a four-leaf clover, if desired). When finished, add stem with plain tube. Practice making shamrocks on waxed paper until you're satisfied with results. Then pipe shamrocks onto cake.

To pipe half-roses: Half-roses are made by piping a mound of icing which is then covered with petals piped one over the other from alternate sides. Begin by holding filled bag as described above. With tube parallel to waxed paper and barely touching surface, pipe a mound of frosting for inside of flower.

To pipe petals: Hold tube so wide end is at base of mound and narrow end is pointing to right, as illustrated. Exert pressure and move from right to left, with wide end of tube acting as a pivot. When petal covers mound, stop pressure and lift off. Then reverse direction, holding tube the same

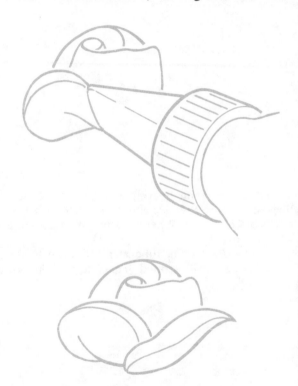

way, with wide end at base of mound but with narrow end pointing left this time. Pipe a second petal, this time swinging from left to right. Then pipe two more petals, each from alternate directions. When four petals cover mound, the flower part is completed. Then add receptacle as illustration shows, using a plain tube to force out a small mound of icing. Add stem with plain tube; then add leaves, if desired (see directions following). Practice piping several roses onto waxed paper. Then pipe them onto cakes as desired.

4. **Leaf tubes** are available in fewer numbers than the others, because their purposes are so specialized. But you can vary the kind of leaves you make simply by varying the length of piping time, pressure, or tube movement. Ruffled leaves, for example, are easily made by using a slight back-and-forth movement with tube as icing is being piped.

To make a leaf: Hold tube at a 45° angle as illustrated, with bag held between second and third fingers as described above. Tip of tube should be almost touching surface. Exert pressure, meanwhile pulling tube away slightly and drawing tube upward slightly to make a point at tip of leaf. Realistic-looking leaves can be made by exerting slightly more pressure at the beginning and relaxing as you near the end of the leaf. Practice piping leaves onto waxed paper until satisfied. Then pipe them onto cake.

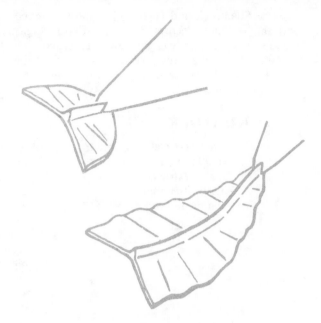

Design cake decorations.

1. Once you have mastered a few simple pastry tube techniques, you'll be ready to design your own cakes. Begin by studying catalogs or cake-decorating books in the library. Look in bakery show windows, florist windows, and flower catalogs. Then try to find tubes in catalogs that will make the desired flowers or shapes. Remember, you can imitate nature if you wish; but you are just as free to pipe strange flowers and colors never seen in nature.

2. Plan design on paper first, indicating the colors and tubes you wish to use. Make the whole design on waxed paper beforehand, if you wish.

Don't try to improvise right onto a cake top until you have experience.

Instructions for making a parchment pastry bag

1. Cut a 24×17×7-inch triangle from baking parchment. Bring points A and B together as illustrated.

2. Bring C around so that A, B, and C meet as in illustration.

3. Fold point ABC into cone.

4. Cut a tab in rim as in illustration; fold tab outward.

Trim 1/2 to 3/4 inch from tip.

5. Insert pastry tube into tip; fill bag half full. Fold down top edges.

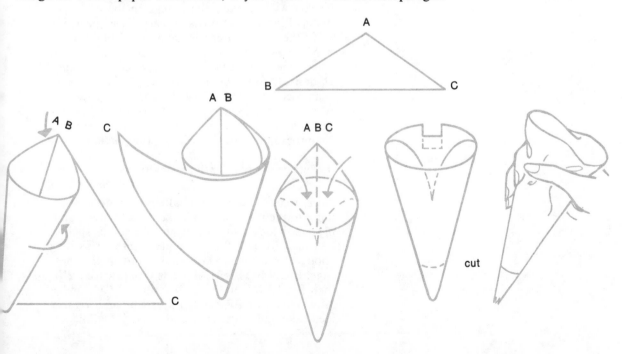

The Shamrock and Heart cakes were designed with the beginning decorator in mind. Extra icing is made so practice piping can be done. To practice or to check the results a tube will give, just fill a tube with icing, hold between finger and thumb, and press icing out with index finger. This will give you an idea of the size and shape of the piping that the tube makes without filling a pastry bag. These cakes may be decorated entirely using just tubes, or with a tube and pastry bag.

●

Shamrock Cake

White Sheet Cake (page 34; use vanilla extract instead of lemon extract)
White Buttercream
Green paste food coloring

1. Trace shamrock and stem patterns on page 66 onto transparent paper. Cut out pieces and lay on half of sheet cake (see illustration).
2. With a small, serrated knife, cut carefully around shamrock and stem. Cut out another shamrock and stem on other half of sheet cake.
3. Place 1 cake layer (a shamrock and a stem) on a serving plate. Prepare icing and join the cake pieces. Tint 4 cups of the frosting very pale green and reserve remaining frosting.
4. Cover top of first layer with pale green icing. Place second layer on frosted layer. Cover top and sides of cake with remaining green icing. Smooth top and sides with a large, flat knife blade or metal spatula dipped in very hot water. Refrigerate cake several hours, or until surface is no longer sticky, before decorating.
5. Tint remaining white icing to make a deep bright green (dark enough to show up against pale green frosting on cake). Refrigerate icing several hours until cake is ready to be decorated.
6. When cake surface no longer feels sticky, it is ready to be decorated. Remove icing from refrigerator and bring to room temperature, or beat with an electric mixer to soften.
7. To decorate cake, use a wooden pick to print ERIN GO BRAGH (Ireland Forever) on cake in block letters about ¾ inch long and ½ inch wide. (If you wish to raise the letters on the cake, see Note.) Pipe letters on cake (instructions, page 57), using the green butter icing and tube 1 or 2 (plain).
8. Make a shell border around bottom edge of cake, using tube 14 or 15 (star) and the green butter icing. If desired, use tube 120 (curved flower) to pipe shamrocks onto cake (instructions, page 58). Tiny whole shamrocks may be made with tube 221, the same way rosettes are made. Place stems on shamrocks, using tube 2 (plain), (instructions, page 58).
9. Refrigerate cake until serving time.

1 shamrock cake

Note: Raised letters on a cake give added importance to the message. To make raised letters, simply slice a long, thin strip from cake scraps slightly less than ½ inch thick. Divide it into strips long enough to accommodate each word in the message. ERIN GO BRAGH needs three strips; a 2½-inch for ERIN, a 1½-inch strip for GO, and a 3-inch strip for BRAGH. Lay strips on a freshly iced cake and cover strips with icing. Outline letters on raised portions with a wooden pick, and cover with lines of rosettes as directed for decorating directly on cake.

White Buttercream

2½ cups sugar
1 cup water
2½ tablespoons corn syrup
¼ teaspoon cream of tartar
¼ teaspoon salt
5 egg whites
4 teaspoons vanilla extract
½ teaspoon almond extract
1⅔ cups butter

1. In a heavy saucepan combine sugar, water, corn syrup, cream of tartar, and salt. Cover and simmer gently for 5 minutes.
2. Remove cover and cook until syrup reaches 246°F.
3. Beat egg whites at high speed until stiff but not dry. While still beating, pour the hot syrup into egg whites in a thin, steady stream. After all the syrup has been added, continue beating 2 or 3 minutes, or until frosting stiffens a little. Add extracts and continue beating until well mixed.
4. Beat 1⅔ cups butter until very soft. Add the icing, ¼ cup at a time, beating well after each addition. Cover and refrigerate until ready to use.

5½ cups

Heart Cake

White sheet Cake (page 34; use vanilla extract instead of lemon extract)
White Buttercream (page 61)
Rose and red paste food coloring

1. Trace heart pattern on page 67 onto transparent paper. Cut out pieces and lay on half of sheet cake.
2. With a small, serrated knife, cut carefully around heart, making one layer. Repeat on other half of sheet cake, making a second layer.
3. Prepare buttercream. Stir a very small amount of rose food coloring into 4 cups of the icing to make a very pale pink. Refrigerate remaining white frosting.
4. Place 1 cake layer on a serving plate. Spread top with pink icing. Set other layer on top and cover top and sides of cake with remaining pink icing. Smooth top and sides of cake with a large flat knife or metal spatula dipped in very hot water. Refrigerate cake several hours, or until no longer sticky, before decoratring.
5. When cake surface no longer feels sticky, remove from refrigerator. Set icing out and bring to room temperature, or beat with electric mixer to soften.
6. Using a wooden pick, mark VALENTINE BE MINE on top of cake, in ¾-inch-high and ½-inch-wide block letters. Pipe letters on cake (instructions, page 57), using white frosting and tube 1 or 2 (plain). (If raised letters are desired, see Note following Shamrock Cake, page 60).
7. Using tube 14 or 15 (star) and white frosting, pipe a shell border (instructions, page 76) along top edge of cake, around base of cake, and down center front (see photo).
8. Refrigerate cake until serving time.

1 heart cake

This cake is the delight of doll-loving girls, not only because they like to look at it and eat it, but also because it can become other dolls simply by changing the decoration.

1. Make a Bride Doll by adding a bouquet of tiny icing roses (instructions, page 58) and affixing a tiny square of net to head with icing.

2. Make a Cinderella Doll by tinting the skirt pink and dividing it into panels with lavender strips. Decorate panels with lavender rosettes and tiny green stems and leaves. Use tube 13 for rosettes, tube 1 for stems, and use tube 16 for the strips between panels.

3. Make a Mother Nature doll by piping large flowers onto the skirt from bottom, so they look like they're growing right up the skirt. Add different-color rosettes for flower heads. Use tube 4 (plain) for stems, tube 18 for flowers, and tube 68 for leaves. Make the bodice green.

●

Snow Queen Doll Cake

Doll Cake
White Buttercream (pge 61)

1. A china (or plastic) doll head and bust will be needed.

2. Lay the 8-inch sponge cake layer on a serving plate. With a long, sharp, serrated knife, split bowl-cake into 2 layers and set aside.

3. Prepare buttercream and spread over top and sides of cake layer on plate. Lay bottom half of bowl-cake over frosted layer and spread with icing; top with upper layer of bowl-cake and cover with icing. Meanwhile, with cupcake upside down, press doll torso into it carefully until doll stands without support.

4. Set cupcake (with doll) on top of cake and cover cake with frosting, using more frosting to keep doll upright, if necessary. Smooth frosting over sides of cake and assemble the skirt, using a spatula dipped often in hot water to make skirt as smooth as possible.

5. Drop tube 28 or 29 (star) into a pastry bag and fill bag with buttercream. Pipe stars over entire surface, starting at top and piping straight rows all the way to base of cake. Stars should touch but not be crowded.

6. Remove pastry tube from bag and drop tube 14 or 15 (star) into bag. Fill again with icing and pipe a border row of shells around bottom of dress. Refrigerate until serving time.

1 Snow Queen Doll Cake

Doll Cake

5 **egg yolks**
1¼ **cups sugar**
⅓ **cup water**
1¼ **teaspoons vanilla extract**

1. Beat egg yolks, half of the sugar, water, and vanilla extract together in large bowl of an electric mixer until very thick. Sift flour over batter and fold in carefully.

1¼ cups sifted cake flour
5 egg whites
½ teaspoon cream of tartar
1/8 teaspoon salt

2. Beat egg whites with cream of tartar and salt until they form soft peaks. With beaters still running, add remaining sugar gradually, continuing to beat until meringue is thick. Fold into batter.

3. Grease the bottom and sides of an 8-inch round layer cake pan and line it on the bottom with greased parchment paper. Grease a 1½-quart oven-proof bowl (7 to 8 inches in diameter at top) and a 6-ounce glass custard cup. Cut small parchment paper rounds to fit in bottom of each; grease the parchment paper and put in place.

4. Divide the batter (there should be about 8¼ cups) into pans as follows: 4 cups into bowl, ⅔ cup into custard cup, and remaining batter into cake pan.

5. Bake at 350°F 25 minutes. Then lay a piece of foil over top of bowl and remove custard cup from oven. Allow another 10 minutes in oven for cake layer (a total of 35 minutes) and allow another 20 minutes for bowl cake (a total of 45 minutes). Cool cupcake upright on wire rack 10 minutes.

6. With a knife, loosen cake from custard cup and turn out on wire rack. Remove paper and finish cooling. Turn layer cake pan and bowl upside down on wire racks to cool as they come from the oven. Do not remove cakes from pans until they fall out by themselves or until they have cooled enough to be loosened easily from sides. Peel off paper, and cool completely.

This cake is especially popular with kindergarten-age girls. It not only looks adorable, but the cake and icing combination is delicious. Icing is spread on the face, hand, and leg areas and piped through a star tube to cover the rest of the cake. Additional decorating includes marshmallows, gumdrops, and marzipan.

●

Rag Doll Cake

White Sheet Cake (page 34; use vanilla extract instead of lemon extract)
White Buttercream (page 61)
Red, blue, and yellow paste food coloring
1½ ounces dark sweet chocolate, melted
2 white cream patties
2 large marshmallows
15 miniature marshmallows
2 large black gumdrops
2 large red gumdrops
1 stick black licorice, soft enough to bend easily (optional)
Marzipan (page 43)

1. Trace head, body, and leg patterns on page 65 onto transparent paper. Cut out pieces and lay on inverted sheet cake (see illustration).

2. Using a small serrated knife, carefully cut around head, body, and legs. Use a metal spatula to transfer cake pieces to a large serving platter or piece of corrugated cardboard covered with aluminum foil.

3. Prepare double recipe of White Buttercream, using frosting to join pieces.

4. Tint 1⅔ cups icing with red food coloring (see page 42 for instructions on using food coloring) to make extremely pale pink for skin. Tint 3⅓ cups icing bright blue for dress. Tint 2 cups icing bright yellow for hair. Stir melted chocolate into remaining icing.

(cont.)

5. Using a metal spatula, spread pink icing over face area. Do not cover sides of face with pink icing as yellow icing will cover it. Cover hands and legs with pink icing, also (see illustration). Smooth icing, using a knife dipped in hot water.

6. Using tube 18, pipe blue stars (instructions, page 57) over entire surface of dress area. Cover both top and sides, placing stars close together, so that no cake shows through.

7. Spread yellow icing over entire surface of doll's head. Using tube 18, a clean pastry bag, and the chocolate icing, cover shoe area with stars.

8. Cut miniature marshmallow in half and arrange, cut side down, at wrists, neck, and down center of doll (see illustration). Lay large marshmallow on skirt of dress and arrange petals made from another large marshmallow to form flower (see photo).

9. To decorate face, place cream patties to form rounds for eyes. Set black gumdrops in center of each patty to complete eyes.

10. Flatten red gumdrops and cut into a triangle for nose, circles for cheeks, and into a thin strip for mouth. If desired, cut very thin strips from a licorice stick for eyebrows and eyelashes.

11. Make marzipan for hair, kneading in enough food coloring to make bright yellow. Fill a garlic press with a small amount of yellow marzipan. Press marzipan into long, thin strings. Use a sharp knife to scrape strings off outside of press and place them on yellow icing forming doll's hair. Continue pressing marzipan and placing strings on sides of head and around the face until yellow icing is completely covered.

12. Refrigerate cake until serving time.

1 doll cake

Clown Cake: Follow directions for Rag Doll Cake through step 3. Leave icing to be used for skin white. Tint icing bright blue for costume. Tint icing for shoes and hair bright red. Outline dress area with some of the blue icing, tinted a little darker, to form pantaloons. Cover cake with icing as directed for Rag Doll Cake. Do not make marshmallow flowers, but place marshmallow slices at random on costume to form spots. Tint marzipan for hair bright red. Using marshmallows, licorice, and gumdrops, decorate face to make either a happy or sad clown.

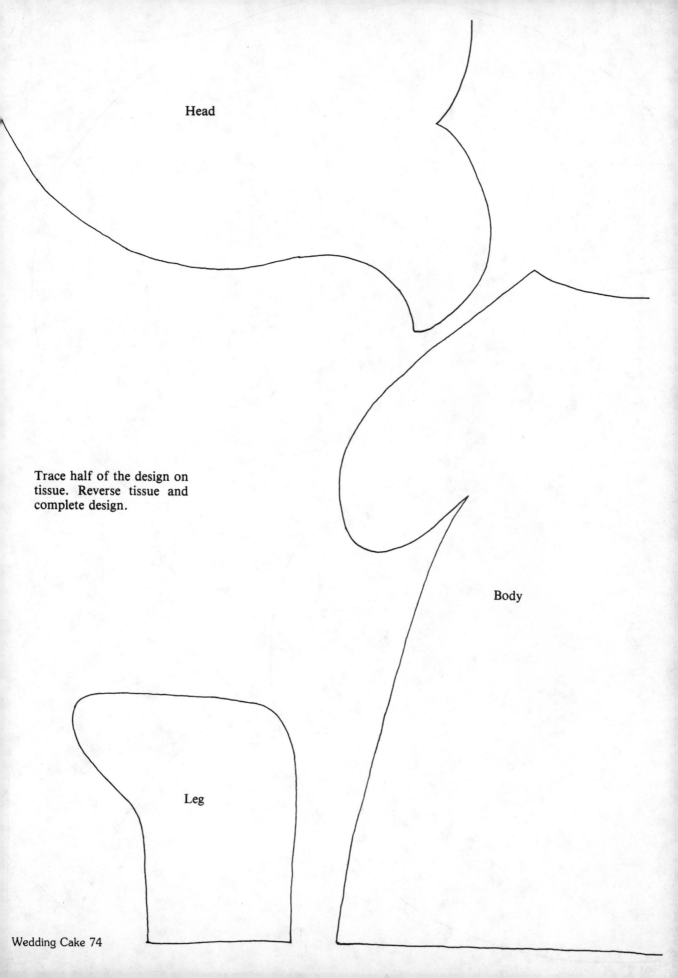

Head

Trace half of the design on
tissue. Reverse tissue and
complete design.

Body

Leg

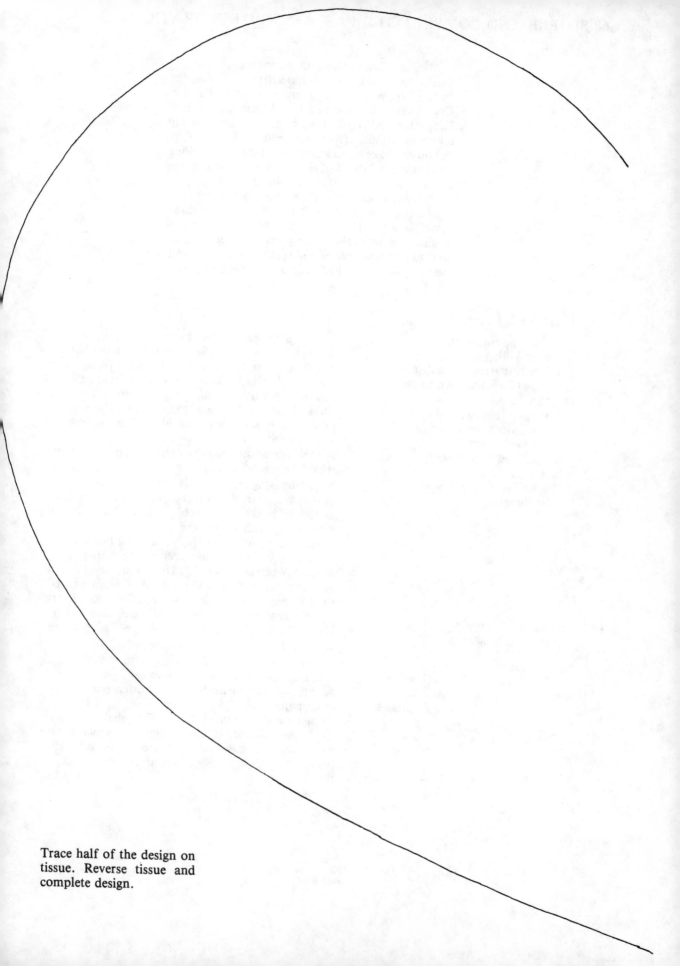

Trace half of the design on
tissue. Reverse tissue and
complete design.

Basket Cakes range in effect from charming (when filled with fresh raspberries) to spectacular (when topped with marzipan strawberries, Crystallized Strawberries, or Mock Crystallized Grapes). Good results are not hard to get, but will take a little time, effort, and beforehand planning.

You can bake the cake and make the cream filling up to two days ahead of time. If you wish to fill the basket with Crystallized Strawberries or Grapes, they must be done only a few hours before serving.

Basket Cakes can actually be filled with anything beautiful or complementary in taste; from meringue mushrooms with chocolate pastry cream decorations to marzipan leaves and roses in any color you choose. You are limited only by your imagination.

●

Basket Cake

Feather Sponge Cake
Cream Filling
White Buttercream (page 61)
2 ounces (2 squares) semisweet chocolate
Marzipan (page 43)
Green paste food coloring
Red tinted sugar
Crystallized Strawberries (optional)
Mock Crystallized Grapes (optional)

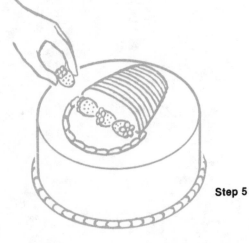

Step 5

Step 6

1. Use a long, serrated knife to slice each cake layer in half horizontally. Lay 1 cake layer half on a serving plate and cover with cream filling. Top with another layer and cover with cream filling. Continue with remaining layers. Frost top and sides of cake with White Buttercream. Dip a decorating comb in hot water, shake off excess drops, and "comb" cake sides evenly.

2. Melt chocolate. Add to remaining buttercream. Blend well; refrigerate.

3. Divide Marzipan in half. Press one half into a basket shape which is 4 inches long, 2½ inches wide at top of basket, 1½ inches wide at base, 1 inch high at top with a flattened base.

4. Add green food coloring to about 2 tablespoons marzipan for leaves. Shape remaining marzipan into 6 strawberries (page 52). If desired, Crystallized Strawberries or Mock Crystallized Grapes can be used in place of marzipan strawberries. Roll marzipan strawberries in red sugar; coat thoroughly. Using tube 67 (leaf), pipe leaves onto each strawberry.

5. Place basket-shaped marzipan on top of cake. Lay marzipan strawberries on cake.

6. Spread chocolate-flavored buttercream over marzipan basket. Then pipe weaving over basket, using tube 19 (see illustration). Pine shells on cake for basket handle. Using a large pastry bag filled with chocolate-flavored buttercream and tube 19, pipe a shell border around bottom of cake.

1 basket cake

Feather Sponge Cake

1²/₃ cups sifted cake flour
¼ teaspoon salt
3 egg yolks
½ cup cold water
1½ cups sugar
1 teaspoon orange extract
½ teaspoon lemon extract
3 egg whites
¾ teaspoon cream of tartar

1. Sift flour and salt together. Set aside.
2. In a large mixing bowl, beat egg yolks until very thick. Add water; continue beating until mixture is very light. Gradually add sugar and extracts. Fold in flour and salt.
3. In a separate bowl, beat egg whites until frothy; add cream of tartar and beat until soft peaks are formed.
4. Fold yolk mixture into egg whites.
5. Spoon batter into two 10-inch round layer cake pans which have been lined on the bottom with greased parchment paper.
6. Bake at 325°F 25 to 30 minutes, or until cake tests done.
7. Invert cakes onto wire racks to cool. Peel off paper. When cake is cool, remove from pans.

Cream Filling

¼ cup cold milk
2 tablespoons cornstarch
4 egg yolks
¾ cup sugar
1/8 teaspoon salt
1¾ cups milk, scalded
2½ teaspoons unflavored gelatin
5 teaspoons water
1½ teaspoons vanilla extract
½ cup whipping cream

1. Mix cold milk with cornstarch in a small bowl, using a wire whisk so that no lumps remain.
2. Mix egg yolks, sugar, and salt in a small, heavy saucepan. Add hot milk to egg yolk mixture, a little at a time, stirring constantly until well combined. Set over low heat and stir in cornstarch mixture. Cook and stir 4 or 5 minutes, or until custard thickens and coats the spoon. Remove from heat.
3. Meanwhile, soften gelatin in water in top of a double boiler, then set over boiling water until melted. Stir gelatin into hot custard and mix well. Then set custard aside to cool, stirring often to allow steam to escape so custard will not become watery.
4. When cool, stir in vanilla extract. Whip cream and fold into custard. Spoon custard into a covered container and store in refrigerator until needed.

Crystallized Strawberries

2²/₃ cups sugar
1 cup water
¼ teaspoon cream of tartar
2 quarts strawberries, rinsed and dried (do not hull); at room temperature

1. Combine sugar, water, and cream of tartar in a small, heavy saucepan and cook without stirring over low heat until candy thermometer registers 300°F. Immediately remove pan from heat and place it in a pan filled with cold water to stop the cooking.
2. Then set pan in a pot filled with boiling water to keep it hot. Spear a strawberry through its hull with a fork (try to use a two-pronged seafood fork, if possible) and dip it into the glazing syrup, turning it until well coated.
3. Remove fruit from fork (don't use fingers) and set on an oiled wire rack to drain and dry.
Note: Other fruits can be crystallized, such as pit-

ted cherries, prunes, dates, etc. Strawberries, which unfortunately are the most beautiful when glazed, contain so much acid that they won't hold up unless made just a few hours (three or four perhaps) before serving. Other fruits, however, will hold up longer.

Mock Crystallized Grapes

1 pound seedless grapes, washed, dried, and cut in very small clusters
3 egg whites, beaten until very frothy, but not stiff
1½ cups superfine sugar

1. Dip grape clusters, one at a time, into egg white, coating well on all sides. Let drip and drain for a moment (shake them lightly) until excess egg white runs off.
2. Dip a grape cluster into sugar, coating well on all sides. Set on an oiled wire rack to dry. Repeat with remaining grape clusters.
3. Pour remaining sugar, a little at a time, through a strainer held over grapes on wire rack. Scrape excess sugar into bowl and pour it through again, until grapes are well coated. Allow to dry thoroughly, then chill. Use to garnish top of basket cake, but do not add them until the last minute before serving.

Note: Mock Crystallized Grapes can be made the day before serving. Cover and refrigerate.

Little Frosted Cakes provide a great oppotunity for perfecting decorating techniques or creating original designs. When decorating small cakes, just remember that the decorating should be in proportion to the size of the cake. Decorating several small cakes usually takes a little longer than decorating one large cake, but if only tubes are used it is quicker than having to fill a pastry bag each time the tube is changed. Having many little cakes to decorate will give you much creative pleasure, and will bring admiring comments each time you serve them.

Little Frosted Cakes

Square Cocoa Cake
1 cup sieved raspberry jam
Poured Chocolate Icing
Square White Cake
Fondant Glaze or White Buttercream (pages 51, 73)
Paste food color

1. With chocolate cake upside down, cut it into sixteen 2-inch squares. Cover each 2-inch square with sieved raspberry jam, using about 1 tablespoon per cake to cover top and sides. Set jam-covered cakes about 1 inch apart on wire rack and place in refrigerator to chill while making poured icing.
2. When icing is ready, remove cakes from refrig-

erator and place rack over a large baking sheet with sides. Slowly pour hot icing in a very thin stream over top of one cake, letting it run down the sides. Repeat with remaining cakes. When tops are well covered, use a wide spatula to scoop up icing that has collected on bottom of baking sheet, and cover any places on sides of cake that are bare of icing.

3. Reserve 2 tablespoons chocolate icing from bottom of baking sheet to mix with buttercream later. Then refrigerate iced chocolate cakes until ready to decorate with buttercream.

4. Invert white cake upside down, cut it into sixteen 2-inch squares.

5. Pour Fondant Glaze over squares or take 5½ cups White Buttercream from refrigerator and put into separate bowls as follows:

    (a) Put 1 cup buttercream into first bowl and reserve.

    (b) Put 1 cup plus 2 tablespoons buttercream into second bowl and add yellow paste color to make a pale yellow.

    (c) Put 1 cup plus 2 tablespoons buttercream into a third bowl and add violet or blue paste color to make a pale lavender.

    (d) Put 1 cup plus 2 tablespoons buttercream into a fourth bowl and add rose paste color to make a pale pink.

    (e) Put ½ cup buttercream into a fifth bowl and add green paste color to make a medium emerald green.

    (f) Put ½ cup buttercream into a sixth bowl. Set the 2 tablespoons reserved chocolate icing in a small pan over low heat and stir until softened. Mix with buttercream.

Place green and chocolate buttercreams in refrigerator until ready to decorate.

6. Meanwhile, frost white cakes as follows:

    (a) Cover top and sides of 4 cakes with uncolored buttercream, using about 2 tablespoons per cake, or slightly more if needed. Set aside remaining buttercream.

    (b) Frost top and sides of 4 cakes with yellow buttercream as above.

    (c) Frost top and sides of 4 cakes with violet buttercream as above.

    (d) Frost top and sides of 4 cakes with rose buttercream as above.

You will have 32 cakes: 16 chocolate, 4 white, 4 yellow, 4 violet, and 4 rose colored.

7. Refrigerate cakes and remaining buttercream until set. When ready to decorate, remove buttercreams from refrigerator and allow to soften slightly.

8. Meanwhile, assemble pastry tubes and examine the different suggested ways of decorating cakes, or make up your own designs. Remove cakes from refrigerator and decorate.

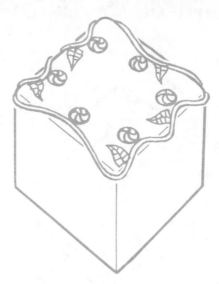

9. *Illustration 1:* Fill tube 2 (plain) with green icing and pipe a wavy "stem" line (instructions, page 59) around top of cake as pictured. With same tube, add tiny lines for leaves or tendrils. Fill a tube 14

(star) with any color icing except green and pipe several tiny rosettes (instructions, page 58) onto stem. Repeat, using other colors for rosettes, if desired.

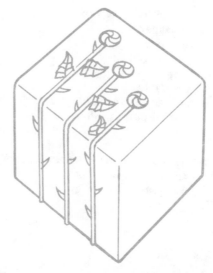

10. *Illustration 2:* Fill a tube 30 (star) with any color icing desired (except green) and pipe 3 rosettes (in-

structions, page 58) on an angle as pictured. (Or, use a different color icing for each rosette, if desired.) Fill a tube 2 (plain) with green icing and pipe straight-line "stems" (instructions, page 58) parallel to each other across top and down one side as pictured. Add short straight lines, using same tube for leaves and tendrils. Or, if desired, fill tube 65 (leaf) with green icing and make a few small leaves for each "stem".

11. *Illustration 3:* Use any color icing but green to fill a tube 104 (straight flower) and pipe a half-rose (instructions, page 58) in center of cake. Fill a tube 2 with green icing and pipe a mound for receptacle (enlarged part of stem at base of flower). Then pipe a small stem (instructions, page 58). Fill a tube 67 (leaf) with green icing and pipe a leaf or two (instructions, page 59) as desired.

Square White Cake

1½ **cups sifted all-purpose flour**
1 **cup sugar**
2 **teaspoons baking powder**
¼ **teaspoon salt**
¼ **cup lard**
1 **egg, beaten**
¾ **cup milk**
½ **teaspoon vanilla extract**

1. Grease bottom of a 9-inch square baking pan. Line bottom with waxed paper and grease paper; set aside.
2. Sift flour, sugar, baking powder, and salt together in a bowl and mix. Cut in lard with a pastry blender or two knives until particles resemble rice kernels.
3. Add a mixture of egg, milk, and vanilla extract, mixing until all ingredients are moistened. Turn batter into prepared pan.
4. Bake at 375°F 30 minutes, or until cake tests done. Cool in pan on wire rack 10 minutes. Turn out of pan and peel off paper. Cool completely.

One 9-inch square cake

Square Cocoa Cake

1⅓ **cups sifted cake flour**
1 **cup sugar**
½ **cup cocoa**
1 **teaspoon baking powder**
½ **teaspoon baking soda**
¼ **teaspoon salt**
6 **tablespoons vegetable shortening or all-purpose shortening**
2 **eggs**
¼ **cup milk**
1½ **teaspoons vanilla extract**
½ **cup milk**
2 **teaspoons cider vinegar**

1. Grease a 9-inch square baking pan. Line bottom of pan with waxed paper and grease paper; set aside.
2. Sift flour, sugar, cocoa, baking powder, baking soda, and salt together in a large bowl; blend to distribute cocoa. Add shortening.
3. Add a mixture of the eggs, ¼ cup milk, and vanilla extract to dry ingredients. Beat with electric mixer at medium speed 2 minutes (or beat vigorously about 300 strokes). Scrape sides and bottom of bowl occasionally.
4. Add a mixture of ½ cup milk and the vinegar to batter. Beat at medium speed for 1 minute (or beat vigorously about 150 strokes). Turn batter into prepared pan.
5. Bake at 350°F about 30 minutes, or until cake tests done. Cool cake in pan on rack 10 minutes. Loosen sides and turn out on rack, peel off paper, and cool completely.

One 9-inch square cake

Poured Chocolate Icing

¼ teaspoon cornstarch
Pinch salt
1½ cups sugar
¾ cup water
5 ounces (5 squares) unsweetened chocolate
1½ tablespoons butter
¾ teaspoon vanilla extract

1. Mix cornstarch, salt, and sugar together in a small, heavy saucepan. Add water and mix again. Bring to boiling; insert candy thermometer and cook until it registers 236°F.

2. Immediately add chocolate and butter and stir constantly until chocolate has melted completely. Stir in vanilla extract. Use immediately to coat small chocolate cakes.

Note: If icing hardens, reheat over low heat, stirring constantly until pouring consistency.

Fondant Glaze

3 cups sugar
1½ cups water
¼ teaspoon cream of tartar
1 teaspoon vanilla extract
Flavoring or liqueur as desired
Food coloring as desired
Hot water as needed

1. Mix sugar, water, and cream of tartar in a heavy saucepan with a tight-fitting cover. Stir over low heat until sugar is dissolved. Increase heat and bring mixture to boiling. Cover saucepan and boil mixture gently 5 minutes. Uncover and put candy thermometer in place.

2. Continue cooking, without stirring, but wash sugar crystals from sides of saucepan with pastry brush dipped in water. Cook until mixture reaches 238°F (soft-ball stage). Remove pan from heat and remove candy thermometer.

3. Wipe a large smooth level platter, or a flat surface (such as a marble slab) with a damp cloth. Immediately pour syrup onto platter or slab; do not scrape pan. Without stirring, cool syrup to lukewarm, or until just cool enough so platter can be held on hand.

4. Pour vanilla extract onto cooled syrup, and with a wide spatula or wooden spoon work fondant in circles from edges to center until white and creamy. Pile into a mound, cover with a bowl, and allow to rest 20 to 30 minutes.

5. With hands, work fondant (using a kneading motion) until soft and smooth. Store 24 hours in a tightly covered jar to ripen.

6. To use as glaze for small cakes, put ripened fondant in double-boiler top, set over simmering water, and melt fondant, stirring constantly, until candy thermometer registers 135°F (no higher). Blend in, to suit taste, any desired flavoring or liqueur. To tint, blend in food coloring as desired (see page 42 for instructions on using food coloring). If fondant is not thin enough to pour, gradually stir in hot water, 1 teaspoon at a time, until fondant is of pouring consistency.

7. Set cakes to be glazed on a rack over a tray. Quickly pour melted fondant over them. Collect dripped fondant from tray, re-melt, and use again. Repeat until cakes are coated.

About 1¼ pounds fondant

Wedding Cake

Eating a sweet dish to celebrate a happy occasion is a custom that goes back before recorded history. The Romans were the first to bake cakes exclusively for weddings, but their manner of serving differed humorously from ours. After a lavish Roman wedding dinner, a large cake was brought out and shown to the guests. After everyone had seen and admired it, the father of the bride then picked it up and banged it down over the bride's head, causing it to break into many small pieces. The small bits of cake, symbolizing fruitfulness, were then distributed to the guests.

The early Anglo-Saxons served wedding cakes too, but these were brought by the wedding guests rather than furnished by the host. It was customary for each guest to bring a small cake to the feast. When the cakes were all piled one on top of each other, they formed a small mountain of cake. The bride and groom, kissing over this mound of sweetness, were supposed to be assured happiness for life.

One day, a visiting French cook saw the mound of cakes at a wedding and conceived the idea of icing the whole thing together, and then cutting slices out of it. The next development, that of baking large layers and then frosting them together, was a logical culinary step.

Wedding cakes are traditionally white—not only because white stands for purity in western cultures, but also because white traditionally symbolized joy in ancient times. On the other hand, the flowers, or any kind of floral device used to decorate cakes, are symbols of fruitfulness—a wish on the part of all present for the forthcoming union to be fruitful. A groom's cake is popular at the wedding, too. It is either a chocolate cake or a fruit cake.

Traditionally, the bride cuts the first piece of cake. Anyone else doing so would supposedly be "cutting" into her future happiness.

Wedding cakes are personal symbols and should be decorated as the cook sees fit. The following three-tier cake is baked in two 14-inch round layer cake pans (2 inches deep), two 10-inch round layer cake pans (2 inches deep), and two 8-inch round layer cake pans (2 inches deep). Before making the batter, coat all pans with pan-coat (1/2 cup white shortening and 1/4 cup flour).

Our cake uses seven whole recipes of White Cake Batter: Four recipes for the two 14-inch pans; two recipes for the two 10-inch pans; one recipe for the two 8-inch pans.

Cake layers should be baked, cooled, and then covered with undercoat and refrigerated for about one day before assembling, frosting, and decorating the cake.

•

White Cake Batter

    3 **cups sifted cake flour**
    1 **tablespoon baking powder**
  1/2 **teaspoon salt**
  3/4 **cup butter**
    1 **tablespoon vanilla extract**
  1/4 **teaspoon almond extract**
    1 **cup sugar**
  1/2 **cup water**
  1/2 **cup milk**
    6 **egg whites**
  3/4 **cup sugar**

1. Sift together cake flour, baking powder, and salt and set aside.
2. Meanwhile, cream butter and extracts. Add 1 cup sugar gradually, creaming until fluffy after each addition.
3. Mix water and milk. Add dry ingredients in fourths to creamed mixture, alternating with liquid in thirds; beat only until smooth after each addition.
4. In a separate bowl, beat egg whites until frothy; continue beating, adding 3/4 cup sugar gradually and beating until rounded peaks are formed. Spread beaten egg whites over batter and gently but thoroughly fold together.
5. Consult chart for required amount of batter for each size round layer cake pan.
6. Bake at 350°F following baking time in chart.
7. When layers have cooled completely, make Undercoat.

7 cups

SIZE OF PAN	CUPS OF BATTER PER PAN	BAKING TIME
14-inch	14	45 to 50 minutes
10-inch	7	35 to 40 minutes
8-inch	3½	35 to 40 minutes

Undercoat

1⅓ cups butter
3 tablespoons vanilla extract
½ teaspoon almond extract
12 cups sifted confectioners' sugar (about 1⅔ pounds)
2 egg whites
¼ to ¾ cup cream

1. Cream butter and extracts until fluffy. Alternately add confectioners' sugar, egg white, and cream, beating well after each addition. Beat until smooth and of spreading consistency.
2. Spread the Undercoat thinly on tops and sides of cooled cake layers to seal and to help keep the cake moist and fresh.
3. Cover each layer well with waxed paper, tucking paper under wire rack. Refrigerate layers until ready to assemble. Under no condition put layers together while being stored; Undercoat will harden and layers will stick together.

7 cups

Decorating Frosting

½ cup butter or margarine
2 teaspoons vanilla extract
6 cups sifted confectioners' sugar
¼ cup warm cream

1. Cream butter and vanilla extract until fluffy.
2. Alternately add confectioners' sugar and cream, beating until smooth.

3 cups

TO ASSEMBLE AND FROST CAKE

1. When ready to assemble cake, cut an 8- and a 10 inch round from cardboard. (Cardboard merely prevents knife from cutting into lower layers.)
2. Meanwhile, prepare 4 recipes of Decorating Frosting.
3. Place a 14-inch cake layer on a 16-inch cake plate. Spread with a little frosting and cover with second layer. In the center of this layer, spread a thin layer of frosting the size of the 10-inch layers, coated surface up. Spread top with frosting; cover with the other 10-inch layer.
4. In the center of the top layer, spread a thin layer of frosting the size of the 8-inch cardboard round. Press cardboard firmly into the frosting. Top with 8-inch layers coated side up.
5. Frost sides of all 3 tiers (layers), completely covering the cake. Dip a spatula in hot water and smooth frosting. Frost exposed top of each tier. Dip a decorating comb in hot water, shake off excess drops, and "comb" cake evenly, top and sides. Refrigerate cake for a few hours.
6. Meanwhile, use some of the remaining frosting to pipe 15 full-blown roses and to practice making shells (see below).

(cont.)

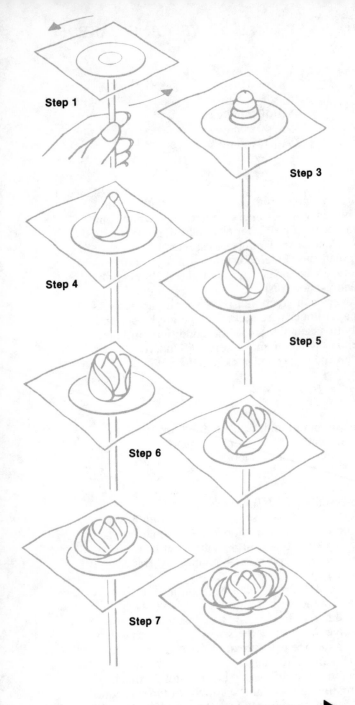

Step 1

Step 3

Step 4

Step 5

Step 6

Step 7

TO MAKE FULL-BLOWN ROSES

1. Cut a square of waxed paper slightly larger than the top of a # 7 flat decorating nail (see illustration) and use a dab of frosting to affix paper to top of nail.

2. Using a pastry bag and tube 104 or 126, fill the bag with frosting.* Hold bag in right hand (if right handed) and nail in left hand.

3. Pipe a small mound of frosting directly into center of waxed paper. This acts as the center of the flower; its size will determine the size of the finished flower—the bigger the mound, the bigger the flower.

4. Place tube narrow end up next to mound, and lean top slightly in toward mound as illustrated. Begin squeezing pastry bag with a steady, even pressure, and as you squeeze, turn nail slowly counterclockwise, until one tight petal has been formed around mound. Petal should be closed and have a tight, curled look, as illustrated.

5. Pipe a second petal in the same manner, starting it a little behind the preceding one and turning nail counterclockwise, as before. Keep this second petal tight, as before, for a closed rosebud look.

6. With large end of tube touching bud at the bottom, pipe a third petal, making it somewhat looser by tilting the upper, narrow end of the tube slightly outward. Then pipe the fourth petal in a similar manner.

7. Pipe several more outside petals in the same open fashion. As you pipe these wider petals, slant the tube away from the flower slightly, to give a rolled back look to each. (A little practice will ensure success.)

8. Carefully remove the waxed paper with frosting flower from the nail and transfer it to a flat baking sheet or tray. In this way, one nail can be used for as many roses as needed. Place baking sheet in freezer until ready to use roses.

---

*If desired, frosting may be tinted pink or yellow.

TO MAKE SHELLS AND SHELL BORDERS ▶

1. Set out a flat tray or plate on which to practice.

2. Using a pastry bag and tube 199 or 32 (large star), fill with frosting. To begin first shell, hold tube at a 60° angle to tray and exert pressure on the bag. As shell enlarges, raise the tube slightly; then immediately begin relaxing pressure and lowering tube. When shell is formed, stop pressure completely.

3. Practice making single shells as in illustration. Then practice making a line of shells, beginning each new one on the "tail" of the last, as illustrated.

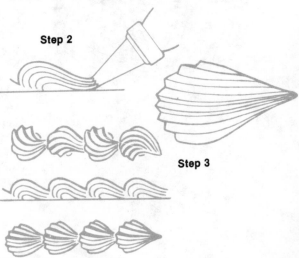

Step 2

Step 3

To Decorate Wedding Cake

1 frosted 3-tiered white cake
  Butter Decorating Frosting
    (page 51)
  Tube 199 or 32 (large star) for
    shell borders and rosette
    flowers
  Tube 16 or 27 (small star) for
    arches
  Tube 4 or any plain tube, for
    stems
  Tube 70 or 67 (leaf) for leaves
  Several pastry bags, and a
    coupling for changing small
    tubes
15 frosting roses
40 to 50 small, real rosebuds with
    short stems for decorating
    plate and top of cake.

To Serve Wedding Cake

Step 1

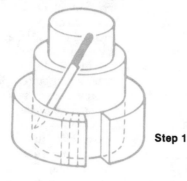

Step 2

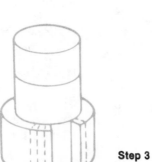

Step 3

1. Examine frosted cake. If any section has sunk, build it up with decorating frosting and smooth out surface, using decorating comb to make necessary repairs. It is essential that cake top be as smooth and uniform as possible.

2. Pipe a shell border around bottom of cake, following directions on page 76. Then pipe shell borders around bottom of middle layer, and around bottom of smallest layer as in photograph.

3. Using a pastry bag and tube 16 or 27 (small star), fill with frosting. Pipe 5 equal-sized rosette arches (with even amounts of space between each) on bottom layer. Then pipe 5 equal-size arches on middle layer, lining them up with those on lower tier, but making them slightly smaller on the smaller layer, as in photograph. If desired, pipe tiny arches on top layer, or decorate only with bunches of rosette flowers, stems, and leaves. If desired, pipe double arches.

4. Using same large star tube as for shell borders, pipe 3 rosette flowers between sides of arches as pictured. Using tube 4 (plain), make a stem for each flower. Pipe shell borders with large star tube at top of 8-, 10-, and 14-inch cake layers. If desired, make reverse shells. Do so by following instructions for shells, but circle right before easing pressure. Repeat, circling left.

5. Using tube 70 (leaf), make leaves as illustrated, 2 on each side of rosette flower stems, and 2 inside each arch for whole roses.

6. With the sharp point of a knife, transfer whole roses to cake sides, affixing them gently to leaves, and letting the shell border underneath act as a partial support (see photo). Refrigerate cake until ready to serve.

7. At serving time, decorate top of cake with 2 rosebuds. Then border exposed rim of cake plate with rosebuds as in photo.

TO SERVE WEDDING CAKE

1. Hold knife vertically and cut through the bottom layer around outside of middle layer as illustrated. Slice part of bottom layer that extends beyond middle layer into serving-size pieces.

2. Repeat with middle layer, as illustrated, cutting through middle layer around outside of top layer only to top of bottom layer.

3. Top layer may be removed and placed on a small serving plate on the table. The bride and groom often take the top layer home and freeze it, so that they may enjoy it on their first anniversary. Remainder of the cake may be removed to the kitchen for slicing. Serve on individual plates or from one large plate. It is best to wipe crumbs and frosting from the knife frequently. Dipping the knife in hot water also aids in cutting the cake.

120 servings

Index